creative containers

creative containers

Paul Williams Special photography by Georgia Glynn Smith

conran
OCTOPUS

First published in 1997 by Conran Octopus Limited
a part of Octopus Publishing Group Ltd
2–4 Heron Quays
London E14 4JP

www.conran-octopus.co.uk

Reprinted 1997

This paperback edition published in 2001

COMMISSIONING EDITOR Stuart Cooper
PROJECT EDITOR Helen Ridge
ASSISTANT EDITOR Tessa Clayton
COPY EDITORS Sarah Sears, Anne de Verteuil
ART EDITOR Sue Storey
SPECIAL PROJECTS PHOTOGRAPHED BY Georgia Glynn Smith
PICTURE RESEARCH Julia Pashley
PRODUCTION Sue Bayliss

A catalogue record for this book is available from the British Library

ISBN 1 84091 250 2

Printed and bound in China

Page 1: Simple planting in unusual containers, such as these cone-shaped wicker baskets, successfully
breaks up a dull expanse of fence or wall.

Pages 2–3: The assortment of containers and plants lining this path brings a welcome burst of colour.

Page 5: The light and airy conditions offered by a balcony are ideal for growing trailing plants and fruits.
Even a small trough will yield a generous crop of strawberries.

Contents

Introduction

Container gardening is, above all, about flexibility: whether you are gardening in vast acres or on the tiniest of balconies, containers give you the opportunity to introduce colour, shape and texture wherever and whenever they are needed.

All the practical information you will need to create and sustain container planting schemes is given here. Armed with this essential knowledge, you will have the confidence to design your own displays, match plants to containers and place them to best advantage. Appearing at intervals throughout the book is a range of original planting schemes, set out as easy-to-follow practical projects, showing how pots, hanging baskets and windowboxes, as well as improvised containers, can be used to exciting and dramatic effect.

The extensive directory contains all the essential information you will need for the care and cultivation of over 150 plants. It will also encourage you to experiment with more unusual plants, to create your own original container displays.

Containers of colourful flowers can be used to create unexpected surprises in dark corners of the garden. Here, the shadowy background serves to emphasize the brightness of the pelargoniums and felicias as they are caught by the sun's rays.

WHATEVER CONTAINER you choose, whether a custom-made terracotta windowbox or a chipped enamel bucket, a reproduction stone urn, wire hanging basket or an old wooden feeding trough, each has its own advantages and disadvantages. This chapter looks at the best uses of all these materials, helping you to make the most of their special characteristics and thereby enabling you to explore the enormous scope of container gardening. It then examines the huge range of plants you can consider, before supplying all the practical information you will need on composts, drainage, watering and feeding, to ensure that your plants remain healthy and vigorous throughout the growing season.

Materials and Methods

ABOVE: *New terracotta is the perfect surface for painting colourful patterns in emulsion or oil paint.*
LEFT: *Good quality compost, whether soilless or soil-based, will provide the right conditions for strong root growth and healthy container plants.*

TYPES OF CONTAINER

Plant containers come in a wide range of styles and materials, from grand stone urns to earthy hand-thrown terracotta ware, from plain plastic pots to glazed ceramic jars. Inventive gardeners will see potential in all sorts of unlikely objects – an old coal scuttle, a laundry copper, a shiny new dustbin or a kitchen colander.

Every material has its virtues and, as long as it provides good growing conditions, even the most undistinguished-looking container can be planted or decorated to make a big impact. And the simplest decorative techniques will transform the humblest of containers – painting, stencilling or gilding, binding with rope, covering with shells or creating patterns with mosaic tesserae.

TERRACOTTA

Terracotta is a natural material that provides good growing conditions. The porous clay helps to prevent the compost becoming waterlogged and allows air to the roots, while evaporation from the pot helps to keep the roots cool, although this does increase the need for watering. Terracotta is

prone to frost damage but you can minimize the risk by keeping the compost well drained. Always ask whether the pot is frostproof when you buy it.

Although new terracotta can look stark, it will develop a patina. Machine-made pots take longer than hand-thrown ones to do this, but you can accelerate the ageing process by keeping empty pots in a damp, shady place to encourage the growth of greenery or painting them with sour milk or plain yoghurt.

Broken pots can be repaired with adhesive, but, to be more traditional, you can drill a line of holes down each side of the break with a masonry drill, and then tie wire across the break at each matching pair of holes, giving a scar-like effect.

PLASTIC

Plastic containers are inexpensive and available in a wide variety of colours, shapes and styles. Non-porous, plastic keeps compost moist for longer than terracotta, and, generally, the planting itself shades the container and protects the roots from heat damage. Plastic pots can usually be lifted and moved easily if they are filled with peat compost but this does leave the pots less stable.

WOOD

Wooden containers are especially good for insulating roots from extremes of temperature. You can make your own using either pressure-treated timber or planed wood, but the latter will need painting or treating with a plant-friendly preservative. An annual coat of quality car wax will also help prolong their life. You may need to drill drainage holes or use a durable liner inside to prevent the wet compost rotting the wood.

ABOVE: *Olive oil tins, with a simple planting of Petunia 'Brass Band', make cheap and colourful improvised containers.*

FAR LEFT: *Terracotta pots are available in various shapes and sizes, suiting many styles of planting.*

STONE

Stone troughs exude a sense of timeless stability. More elaborate urns, meanwhile, tend to be used more self-consciously as decorative focal points. Reconstructed stone is a cheaper alternative to natural stone and its starkness gradually weathers down – relatively quickly if you treat the surface.

METAL

Painted or left untreated, and planted with strong foliage, metal containers work well in modern, clean-lined gardens, and can add a whimsical touch in a cottage garden setting. Try battered old buckets and troughs as well as shiny new ones.

PLANTS FOR CONTAINERS

Almost all types of garden plant can be grown in containers – shrubs, climbers, hardy and tender perennials, annuals, bulbs, alpines, grasses, fruit, vegetables and herbs. Certain house plants and succulents will also enjoy a summer outdoors, and will provide good foliage to mix with bedding plants in a container.

Container gardening does, in fact, have positive advantages. You can create displays that might be difficult or impossible in a border by grouping plants with different soil requirements in a series

Evergreen box make impressive container plants.
Large established specimens need regular feeding.

of pots. In addition, certain tender plants that would not survive the winter in a border will thrive in pots as they can be moved indoors or to a warmer, sheltered part of the garden.

Container plantings will be more exciting and original if you include some out-of-the-ordinary plants; you can track them down in a publication called *The Plant Finder*, which offers a comprehensive listing of thousands of plants and the nurseries that stock them. Or, even better, visit horticultural shows where specialist growers exhibit and sell new plant specimens.

Experiment with your plantings, too. Do not be put off because you are not sure if a combination will work. If you use your common sense and avoid trying to combine opposing extremes, such as sun-loving plants and those that prefer damp conditions, you will create some exciting and dramatic displays.

SHRUBS

In a large container planting, shrubs can either stand dramatically alone or create a permanent framework around which seasonal interest can be introduced – through perennials, bulbs and annuals. Evergreen shrubs obviously make a year-round contribution, but there are many deciduous shrubs with attractive foliage or stem colour, or an interesting outline shape, that are invaluable for introducing some sort of seasonal variety.

PERENNIALS

Summer-flowering tender perennials, such as osteospermums, pelargoniums and gazanias, are an essential ingredient of container plantings. With their long flowering season, they are invaluable for creating an effect of abundance and are the mainstay of small pots, hanging baskets and windowboxes alike. The terrific range of colours that they offer gives scope for some very dramatic designs. If it is not possible to overwinter them in a conservatory or heated greenhouse (see page 19), you must decide whether to take cuttings to grow on, leave them out and risk the weather, or discard them as annuals.

Hardy perennials do not need winter protection, and will provide interest throughout the growing season – not only with flowers. If planted in autumn or winter, they will signal spring's arrival with colourful new buds of foliage. The emergent growth of euphorbias, peonies and ferns has an intensity of texture and hue probably unmatched in any mature foliage.

Easily grown but tender, sedges make striking architectural displays. Simple, unembellished pots enhance their qualities.

ABOVE: *Exotic fruits, such as lemons, give a distinctive hot-climate feel to a garden.*
FAR RIGHT: *Tulips, available in colours across the spectrum, are among the showiest of bulbs and create a vibrant, late spring display.*

As a hardy plant's flowering season is brief compared with that of a tender perennial, it needs to have good foliage, in order to be equally effective in and out of flower. Hostas, with their distinctively shaped, variegated or textured leaves, are an obvious choice. Combined with grasses such as *Molinia caerulea* 'Variegata' or *Helictotrichon sempervirens*, they have considerable impact.

ANNUALS

Annuals are a cheap and easy way to produce an abundance of colour. Modern hybrids have been bred to produce weatherproof and free-flowering plants. Look out for some unusual subjects in seed catalogues and give them a try.

BULBS

Many bulbs fare better in the sharply drained conditions that pot culture allows than in cold, damp soils. They provide both vibrant colour and a selection of bold and often unusual flower and leaf shapes. Underplanting with bulbs can extend the season of winter plantings and, with careful planning, your display might last from mid-winter to late spring. Beware of using tulips in a winter display that is to be replanted with summer flowers because many tulips are in full flower just when you want to change the planting; use separate pots instead for the tulips and let them flower right through. Feed all spring-flowering bulbs regularly until the leaves die back if you want to keep them for the following year.

DROUGHT-TOLERANT PLANTS

Given the neglect often suffered by plants in containers, drought-tolerant plants make sensible choices, particularly for patios and courtyards, which tend to be sun traps. Use succulents and Mediterranean plants such as *Myrtus communis* (myrtle), *Phlomis fruticosa* (Jerusalem sage) and herbs, which adapt well to hot, dry conditions.

PRACTICAL PLANTING

Over and above ensuring that your plants are provided with the basic growing requirements – light, water and compost – successful container planting is largely a matter of trial and error. You must observe and analyse the performance of your plants throughout the season, familiarizing yourself with their individual needs, in order to acquire the best possible understanding of them – knowledge that will give you the confidence to grow an ever-increasing range.

COMPOSTS

There are essentially two types of growing medium: soil-based and soilless composts.

Traditionally, soil-based composts contain a mixture of sand, loam and fertilizers. They are inherently fertile, releasing their nutrients over a period of time, making them ideally suited to long-term container plantings. Readily rewetted when they become dry, soil-based composts are heavy, which is a disadvantage if you want to move pots around. This can be an advantage, of course, if you have a large or top-heavy planting that is likely to blow over and needs stabilizing. Soil-based composts usually contain lime, so they are not suitable for acid-loving plants, which should be grown in an ericaceous (or acidic) compost.

All soilless composts used to be peat-based, but in response to current ecologicial concerns about the depletion of peat bogs, they are now made from a range of materials, including bark and coir. With no natural nutritional value, all fertilizer has to be added, and plants grown in soilless compost will need feeding right through the season. They are light and easy to handle, however, and combine good water retention with good aeration, provided that the compost is not firmed too much when the containers are planted.

Never pot up plants in garden soil. Not only do you risk importing weed seeds, soil pests and diseases, you are likely to end up with a solid mass of earth that neither water nor air can penetrate.

FEEDING

Nutrients can either be incorporated in the compost before you add your plants or added later, as liquid feed. Slow-release fertilizers, in

Slow-release fertilizer added to soil-based compost will prolong its life for another season.

the form of granules, provide soilless composts with enough nutrients to last the duration of a whole growing season.

Traditional organic equivalents of the slow-release fertilizer are hoof and horn, and bonemeal. Hoof and horn releases nitrogen steadily over a long period, for leafy growth, while bonemeal provides phosphate to stimulate root growth. It can make composts alkaline, however, so do not use it with lime-hating plants like rhododendrons and camellias.

Liquid feeding involves adding plant food to the water at intervals during the growing season. Never add more feed to get a bigger, better plant: too much fertilizer prevents water uptake and the plant may wilt even when the compost is wet.

For quick, if short-lived, results, either use a foliar feed that is sprayed directly onto the leaves, or water an ammonium sulphate solution (6g to 1 litre/1oz to the gallon) onto damp compost, avoiding contact with the foliage. Both supply a nitrogen boost, stimulating lush, green growth.

WATERING

Plant roots need a balance of air and water. Both underwatering and overwatering can upset this balance and cause the plants to suffer. Dry, peat-based composts can be difficult to rewet because once the compost shrinks and cracks, the water simply runs straight through. Either dunk the container in a bowl of water and give it half an hour's soaking or add washing-up liquid to the watering can. This will help the peat to soak up the water. Too regular a use of detergent will deplete the compost's oxygen, so be careful. Meanwhile, the surface of a soil-based compost will, over time, become compacted and crusted with watering, making it equally inefficient as a means of transport for water and air. A layer of organic mulch such as peat, bark or cocoa fibre on the compost's surface will prevent this.

It is easy to assume that pots will not need watering after a good downpour, but foliage can prevent the rain reaching the compost. However, you should certainly collect and use your rainwater, particularly in hard-water areas, where lime from tap water can build up in the compost, making it unsuitable for lime-hating plants. Although you can add granules of sequestered iron to the water to alleviate the problem, prevention is always better than cure.

Most plants should be watered thoroughly, and then left to start getting dry before they are watered again. The most effective method is to pour water gently into the base of a planting – without using a rose. Avoid always watering in the same place, because this can damage the foliage, creating a 'hole' in the display. To reach hanging baskets or awkwardly positioned pots, tie a garden cane to the hose to stiffen the end and give you more control over the watering.

Always soak plants well before planting them. As the roots will not penetrate the new compost for a week or two, it is really important to ensure that water reaches them and not just the surrounding compost.

You can now buy polymer gels which are mixed into a compost to improve its water-retentive capacity, thereby reducing the amount of watering required. The crystals absorb water and swell up to many times their size to form a water reservoir for the plant roots.

This temporary watering system uses strips of disposable kitchen cloth. Move your pots into the shade and out of the wind and place a bucket of water at a level above the pots. From this lead lengths of cloth to each pot and peg them into the compost. Capillary action will siphon a slow trickle of water along the cloth to the pots.

Regular repotting encourages a healthy and vigorous root system that will rapidly send roots into the container compost when planted out.

If you have lots of containers, it may be worth considering an automatic watering device. Systems consist of narrow, connecting pipes that are clipped into individual containers and watering is regulated by a time switch on the garden tap. Controlling the amount of water required and the timing is difficult as container size, plant size and variations in the weather make accurate calculation impossible. A system that uses a moisture-sensitive device pushed into the compost will make the most economic use of water. In hard water areas, lime deposits may block the ends of the drip pipes, so you should check them regularly.

DRAINAGE

Good drainage is vital as too much water in the compost drives out the air and kills the roots. For that reason, you should never leave pots standing in saucers of water.

Plants and bulbs left sitting in wet compost may suffer root-rot and containers full of sodden compost are more likely to crack in a frost. Sit containers on a porous, free-draining surface, such as gravel, or use terracotta feet or a wedge to allow any excess water to drain away.

Broken crocks are often placed in the bottom of a pot to assist drainage. This is not necessary if some of the compost is touching whatever the pot is sitting on. If the container is raised off the ground, however, you will need a layer of gravel or crocks to act as a sump.

POTTING AND REPOTTING

When selecting container plants, consider their mature dimensions, but remember that a plant in a pot has a restricted root zone and so its growth will be limited. Use a container in which a root system sufficiently large to support the plant can develop, or carefully prune the plant to make it smaller and more manageable.

It is generally advisable to renew the compost every year or two – in late winter or early spring, when the plants are dormant. Water the plant the day before repotting as a moist rootball will come out more easily than a dry one. Trim off any visible roots to make it easier to get the rootball out intact. Shake out or wash off some of the soil from the roots, and prune out up to a quarter of them if they are congested, as new roots will grow into the fresh compost. Place the plant in its new pot and feed soil around the roots. Use a stick to prod soil into the spaces between the roots and gently shake the plant as you fill with compost. You may need to top up the compost after one or two waterings.

For a dense container planting, you will need a good volume of compost – for stability as well as moisture and nutrition – so deeper, wider containers are best.

DEADHEADING

Regular deadheading will keep a planting scheme fresh and encourage new flower buds. Cutting off dead leaves with secateurs or scissors takes very little time and, as well as keeping displays tidy, helps prevent infection.

SURVIVING THE WINTER

A wide range of exotic plants can be grown in containers and some will stand a few degrees of frost as long as they are kept almost dry. However, many need to be moved from the garden during the winter months. In exceptionally cold snaps, horticultural fleece, close-woven nylon mesh or newspaper wrapped around tender plants will help protect their leaves.

A temperature just above freezing in a small greenhouse, outhouse or conservatory will see this tender bougainvillea through the winter.

PERHAPS THE MOST EXCITING aspect of designing with plants is the knowledge that the design is only the start; plants will grow into each other in ways that you can never predict. While both the shape of your container and its location may be limiting factors, there is still fantastic scope for imaginative designs, given the incredible variety of plant shapes and habits, flower and foliage colours available. But how do you ensure that your plantings achieve a delicate balance, and that the overall effect doesn't smother the details of individual plants? In looking at combinations of plants in single containers, and combinations of containers in a variety of settings, this chapter will help you to plan successful displays.

Planting Design

ABOVE: *The broad, woolly leaves of Salvia argentea and the fine leaves of the grass illustrate the value of contrasting foliage textures, shapes and colours.*
LEFT: *Clashing colours can create vibrant displays. Here, orange lilies do battle with purple salvias.*

CREATIVE PLANTING

Choosing plants that are arresting or unusual is one method of creating a distinctive planting. Another is to use common plants in unusual ways, such as hostas in hanging baskets or succulents among lush foliage. With well-drained compost and reasonably light and airy conditions you will be able to grow a surprising mixture of plants in the same pot. The art of combining plants lies in using their shapes and colours to contribute to the overall effect, while allowing each plant to retain its own identity.

USING SHAPES

Including plants with a well-defined shape – whether bushy, spiky or arching – will always simplify the process of creating a successful planting. Long-term plantings need a good structure to underpin the more transient, surface layer of flower colour. Plants with bold, upright leaves, arching or trailing stems will help build and define the structure.

Plants with simple, large leaves have a stabilizing effect. Used at the bottom of a group of plants, they create a strong base. Architectural

plants such as melianthus and hedychiums lend themselves to more dramatic arrangements; they have a stately look, which is easily softened by smaller, lighter plants. Single specimens can take the place of ornaments in the garden.

A sense of summer is evoked by using small-leaved flowering plants to create a wispy, 'frizzy' look. But take care not to let a soft, unchallenging planting lose its character or become indistinct. Large, plain leaves will soothe a planting, while spiky and finely cut leaves can jazz it up.

Flowers with distinctive shapes, like abutilons and agapanthus, can bring emphasis to a planting. The number of flowers on a plant and the way they are presented is just as important. The many upright stems of lilac flowers borne by *Nemesia fruticans* create an effect that is as useful as the arching stems and tiny flowerheads of many grasses.

Nevertheless, it is a plant's leaves that have to sustain the display as the flowers come and go around them. It is not difficult to make striking associations with foliage alone, given the astonishing diversity of leaf shape and texture on offer: not just large or small, but huge or tiny, rounded, pointed, ribbed, glossy or furry. A simple but effective rule is always to place plants with dissimilar foliage in adjacent containers, so that each is brought into relief by the other – hostas beside bamboo, for instance.

LEFT: *Foliage plants form the basis of this design with flowering plants added to introduce colour and unify the arrangement.*
RIGHT: *The combination of grey and purple foliage links this container planting with the border plants in a masterly way.*

USING CONTAINERS

There are many different ways of incorporating containers in a garden design: clustered together, in repetitive rows, individually, worked into borders, hanging from trees or pergolas, perched on windowsills or walls – only your imagination limits you. However, it is important to match plants with appropriate containers, and to relate your planting style to the style of your garden.

The inspiration for container plantings may come from a particular part of the garden that you want to decorate and from the feeling or effect you wish to create there. You need to consider how the background will influence the design as you plan: whether the plants will be seen against a wall, a fence, evergreen hedging or larger shrubs in a border. The dark architectural leaves of

Phormium tenax 'Purpureum' will lose much of their strength against dark brick, but will stand out clearly against a busy border. Tall, large-leaved plants, such as hedychiums or zantedeschias, will also help to disguise unattractive backgrounds.

Often the only way to grow plants in small, paved gardens or courtyards or roof gardens is in containers. You can even arrange pots of hardy perennials to resemble a border, moving the plants to the back of the display as they go over.

In every garden there are small microclimates that can be exploited to grow a greater assortment of plants. The spot between the garden wall and the house might be one or two degrees warmer than elsewhere because it gets heat from the house and is sheltered from the wind, so you can grow exotics, such as passion flower and myrtle, without protection. If it has a sunny aspect, you will also be able to exploit the winter sunshine.

It will be cooler and shadier under a tree in summer, but on clear winter nights the branches can also help reduce heat loss from the ground, thereby diminishing the effect of frost.

FORMAL PLANTINGS

The term 'formal garden' probably conjures up images of parterres, knot gardens and grand designs on a large scale, but in fact small gardens lend themselves very readily to formal arrangements. Formality relies for its effect on balance and repetition. To create a look that is strictly formal, use identical containers in rows, each planted with the same type and shape of plant.

The traditional choice for formal planting is evergreen box or yew, clipped into regular shapes. Holly and bay can be grown as standards, although

FAR LEFT: *This witty trio of dwarf sunflowers in terracotta pots lifts the spirits and brightens up the dull brick wall behind.*

LEFT: *This row of repeated box spirals is formal but modern-looking. The irregularity of the top shelf emphasizes the regimented display on the bottom shelves. Clipping box requires patience but results such as this are well worth the effort.*

ABOVE: *Boldly coloured pansies in traditional terracotta pots on an ornamental shelf make a simple yet elegant composition.*

bay will suffer in a cold winter. In a paved garden, set standard plants in rows to make the most of the dramatic shadows they cast, or use their shadows to break up bare areas of wall by placing the containers a little way out from the wall.

A pair of containers, one either side of a doorway, or small pots flanking a flight of steps, create a pleasing symmetry that adds formality to a garden. If the planting is complicated, the container has to be simple with a strong shape to maintain the formal look. Large terracotta pots and Versailles tubs are ideal.

Snow and frost lying on pots arranged in geometric patterns have a striking effect. In summer, on the other hand, you can lighten a formal scheme without detracting from its strength by introducing flowering plants with a single-colour theme.

ABOVE: *A niche cut into the dense foliage of a hornbeam hedge makes a novel setting for a pot of variegated pelargoniums, echeverias and ivy.*
ABOVE RIGHT: *The lush foliage of bamboos, dahlias, salvias and hedychiums can turn a dull backyard into a wonderful jumble of greenery.*

BACKYARD JUNGLES

By choosing a mixture of hardy and tender exotic-looking plants, you can create a jungle in containers outside your back door. Use tall-growing, large-leaved plants such as *Paulownia tomentosa*, *Aralia elata* and *Gunnera chilensis* crowded together to produce a lush, tropical atmosphere. Give these plants as big a root-run as possible to support their exuberant growth; use large containers and feed the plants well. Place showy flowers like cannas, tigridias, *Incarvillea delavayi* and *Vallota speciosa* among them.

ROOF GARDENS

If you live in a top-floor apartment and have access to a strong, flat roof, you can use containers to create a roof garden.

Although a roof garden has the advantage of increased natural light, it is a harsh environment exposed to wind and sun. You can erect trellis windbreaks or use the existing chimney stacks or air-conditioning units as shelter to alleviate the ill effects, and choosing plants suited to dry conditions will help. Use soil-based compost, but beware the extra weight.

Unless there is a barrier around the perimeter, you should secure any pots to prevent them being blown over the edge. Wires stretched between vine eyes, drilled and plugged into any available brickwork, will support climbing plants; the pots themselves could, if necessary, be fixed to them.

CONTAINERS IN BORDERS

Pots nestling in borders so that they are not immediately obvious are like treasures waiting to be found. Stand your pots on clay pipes or stout logs, or set them on a tile or slab to imitate Roman columns with flowerpot 'busts' – particularly effective if repeated along the whole border.

Containers allow you to fill seasonal gaps in borders or make quick alterations to a planting scheme.

Pots on walls, pots in borders, pots in rows, pots on shelves: pots of all shapes and sizes can be carefully arranged in pairs or patterns, or grouped more informally to produce a dramatically different effect every time. Big pots make a big impression, whether planted or empty, but you can make an even bigger one by choosing a large, bold plant with a strong shape as the centrepiece of a grand planting. Collections of small pots, on the other hand, can be used to create a particular theme or colour scheme, even a special mood, in a corner of the garden. Portable, versatile and low-maintenance, and capable of providing the garden with great visual excitement, pots offer the imaginative gardener huge scope.

Pots

ABOVE: *Large, ornate pots can become the focus of a garden room. A planting without the distraction of flowers allows your attention to rest on the container.*
LEFT: *A tiered display of plants invites you to peer closely at the different shapes, colours and textures.*

TYPES OF POT

Pots are available in all shapes and sizes, styles and materials, to suit every kind of garden, whether traditional or modern, formal or informal. If you want to add an individual touch to your planting displays, it is easy to improvise your own pots from recycled household objects.

FLOWERPOTS

The traditional terracotta flowerpot is relatively inexpensive, unbeatably versatile and available in a vast array of sizes, ranging from 2.5cm (1in) to over 90cm (36in) in diameter. Its simple shape makes it ideal for multi-pot displays. Plastic flowerpots are cheaper but less attractive.

PEDESTAL URNS

Pedestal urns have an elegance of proportion that is perfect for formal settings, and which can be enhanced by giving the planting enough height in the centre to balance the height of the pedestal.

Because they hold only a relatively small amount of compost, however, plants near the rim of the urn tend to dry out rather quickly.

VERSAILLES TUBS

Basically square wooden boxes with feet, these are ideal in formal settings planted with individual standard trees and topiary shapes. They are well suited to long-term plantings because they hold a large volume of compost.

LOW, FLAT CONTAINERS

Giving a stable and solid look, this shape works particularly well on paved areas around garden benches where the height of the container is in scale with the seated gardener. Low, squat pots work equally well whether positioned alone or grouped with taller pots. Plants such as tradescantias, *Senecio viravira*, *Bidens ferulifolia*, *Anthemis punctata cupaniana*, *Plectranthus* species and nasturtiums will trail over the edge and along the ground to maintain this horizontal bias.

BULBOUS POTS

In the right position, an empty bulbous pot left on its side makes a useful ornament. But its shape is particularly well suited to full, informal planting, with *Helichrysum petiolare* and *Diascia vigilis* spilling out and down its sides. Placing one amidst a group of straight-sided pots creates a pleasing

LEFT: *Painted wooden containers of clipped box are ideally suited to formal, geometric designs.*
ABOVE RIGHT: *A planting should always be in proportion to the shape and size of its pot; these tall tulips are of just the right size and scale.*

effect too. But there are problems: it is all but impossible to remove large plants for repotting, and, when the compost freezes, round-bellied, narrow-necked pots are prone to crack.

WALL POTS
Wall pots are available in wire, terracotta, plastic and wicker, but you can just as easily use old paint tins. Fix the pots with nails, or use hooks or screws; drill or plug them into the chosen surface.

Wall pots look equally good with a formal or informal planting. A striking effect can be created by planting rows of pots with the same luxuriant scheme, so that the plants spill out and hide the pots completely. Remember that wall pots are usually small and often out of the rain under the eaves, so they tend to dry out quickly.

IMPROVISED POTS
Anything that will hold compost and allows excess water to drain away is a potential plant container. Kitchens, garden sheds and attics are all worth exploring for novel and exciting receptacles ready for a new life: old colanders, cake tins, vegetable baskets, buckets and fruit boxes, tea chests, sinks, milk churns, wire and wicker baskets will all make dramatic new settings for plants. Be adventurous and you will create a highly original focal point.

USING POTS

Just as ornaments can stamp an owner's personality on a house, so small pots can personalize a garden, whether placed singly or in groups. Collections of small pots can 'busy up' dull corners and they are ideal for visually breaking up large expanses of bare wall or paving.

Small container plantings offer great creative scope for playing with different colours, textures and forms. The selection and combination of

*Each pot within a display should have a character of its own. Here, **Lagurus ovatus** and white lobelia combine to create an interesting cameo within a large arrangement.*

plants can be easily altered, and pots rearranged, to suit the changing seasons or to create different moods. Flower colours can range across the whole spectrum, while pots of large-leaved plants such as hostas can be placed close by to act as foils for the bright colours.

A collection of evergreen sempervivums creates a textured pattern of subdued colours and needs only the minimum of attention. When planted singly in pots, or in groups in flat pans, they soon grow to make a mosaic of densely packed rosettes. Neat and compact, these plants are suitable for even the tiniest of containers.

While large pots must be positioned with care to make the greatest impact, there are fewer restrictions governing the placement of small pots. Arranging containers at different heights allows each plant to display its distinct qualities. Simple plantings of a single species placed in lines can be used instead of fences to mark off different areas of the garden.

Large pots allow the gardener to create lavish, bold designs. They lend themselves to large plants with striking leaves and vigorous growth. While still acting as a complement to the garden planting as a whole, these containers will stand in their own right, and, if they contain shrubs or other long-term plants, can be adapted to provide a year-round display. Think of them as you would a piece of garden sculpture and position them where they will make striking focal points. Large pots can be used to dramatic effect on roof terraces or balconies, as their size is more imposing in a confined space, but check first that these areas can actually support the weight of the planted container.

ABOVE: *In time, the* Acaena *'Glauca',* Ajuga reptans *'Atropurpurea',* Lysimachia nummularia *and euonymus in this pot will grow into the border.*
LEFT: *Massing small pots around a larger one creates a richness to compare with a garden border.*

DESIGNING SCHEMES

A planting scheme starts to change the moment you create it and will not reach its full glory until many weeks later. Any planting that is to include a number of different types of plants has an element of unpredictability about it and a big problem for the novice container gardener is knowing how different plants will behave together. What looks to be a nicely balanced planting at the beginning of the season can turn into a lopsided jungle by the end because the original sizes of the plants bear no relation to their eventual heights. Find out as much as you can about about the growth rate and mature size of unfamiliar plants before you start. But remember that a pot-confined plant will grow more slowly than one in the ground.

Use a plant with plenty of character at the centre of a large pot to give structure to the group and to form the body or bulk of the finished planting: melianthus, miscanthus and daturas are good plants for this purpose. Around this central axis, arrange other plants that will complement or contrast, and then add finer, softer foliage plants such as *Lavatera maritima* and *Lotus hirsutus*, which can be tucked in among the larger leaves. The contrast of large leaves with fine leaves, and soft, furry leaves with hard, shiny leaves, will not create the confusing effect you

might expect. Flowers will soften the planting scheme, as well as adding to the colour and richness of the composition.

Trailing plants can be used around the edges to spill attractively over the sides of the pot and, mixed in with the main planting, to create strong horizontal or arching lines; *Helichrysum petiolare* is ideal. *Glechoma hederacea* will give a decisive vertical line to the edge of a planting. Lobelia, bacopas and diascias give a bushy, more luxuriant look, whereas *Felicia petiolata* and *Plectranthus coleoides* 'Variegatus' arch out gracefully.

Stand back and look at the arrangement as you build it and ask yourself questions: Where is the interest? Why am I putting this here? Do I need something tall and graceful or short and squat?

MONOCHROMATIC PLANTINGS

Although often used for miniature alpine gardens, old-fashioned, white ceramic sinks can be planted in more striking ways: one idea is to use a mono-chromatic colour scheme to offset the harsh texture and colour of the sink. A base planting of the black *Ophiopogon planiscapus* 'Nigrescens' might be combined with white hyacinths for the spring and replaced by white *Felicia amelloides* 'Read's White' and white petunias in the summer. The glaze must be kept clean to maintain the scheme's sharp contrasts. A mulch of black stone chippings or coal will stop compost splashing onto the glaze and also tie in with the colour theme.

LEFT: *Simple colour schemes can be very effective, particularly in large-scale plantings.*
RIGHT: *Verbena bonariensis* *tumbles to the ground in this informal scheme of pink and white.*

*In winter, when flowers are in short supply,
plants with strong architectural shapes, such as
yuccas, take on extra importance.*

DRY PLANTINGS

Mediterranean plants, such as *Teucrium fruticans*
(shrubby germander), *Coronilla glauca*, *Lotus
hirsutus*, *Phlomis fruticosa* (Jerusalem sage),
myrtle and rosemary, make strong and characterful mixed summer plantings for small and large
pots alike. They all enjoy hot, dry conditions,
which is ideal, as containers tend to get very dry
in summer. You can develop the Mediterranean
theme: trailing succulents such as *Ceropegia
woodii* and *Lotus berthelotii* will add another
dimension, while stones, pebbles, bleached
driftwood and grit to mulch the top of pots will
emphasize the feeling of dryness.

Otherwise, extend the season of interest with
bulbs that are happy in pots and whose flowers or
leaves suit the dry look, *Nectaroscordum siculum
bulgaricum*, for instance, or *Allium christophii*.
The blue-tinged leaves and soft apricot flowers of
the short *Tulipa batalinii* will both complement
late spring plantings and appreciate a hot baking
in the summer. A plant like *Vallota speciosa*
(Scarborough lily) will finish the season showily.

WINTER PLANTINGS

For winter schemes, use a container that is both
frostproof and rustproof. Choose your plants very
carefully – creative winter planting presents a
real challenge as the main interest must come
from the foliage of evergreen shrubs. There are a
variety of suitable evergreens, such as holly, box,
yew, *Osmanthus delavayi*, *O. heterophyllus* and
Prunus lusitanica. Because growth is slow during
the winter, these plants can be left in their own
pots and plunged into a larger container. Use a
single species of plant, like box, or mix two or
more plants – yew with osmanthus, say – to
emphasize the foliage of each. Underplant with
evergreen ferns such as *Polypodium vulgare* and
dryopteris for another layer of interest.

You need to choose a shrub for the centre of
the pot that tolerates annual pruning in order to
maintain the scale and balance of the design.

Plants with coloured stems, such as *Cornus stolonifera* 'Flaviramea' (yellow-green) or *Salix alba* 'Britzensis' (glowing orange), add a welcome lightness, while ivies trailed over the edge of the pot will help to lessen the slightly stiff look of many evergreens. You could use the fresh greenery of wallflowers to fill any gaps in a winter arrangement and then enjoy their richly coloured, scented flowers in the spring, while underplanting with bulbs – snowdrops and the smaller daffodils – will also bring rewards as the year unfolds.

MAINTENANCE

All container plantings will require maintenance to keep them looking at their best (see pages 16–19), but there are certain tasks that apply particularly to plantings in pots.

No matter how carefully you choose your plants, some will not grow as you originally envisaged. By keeping an eye on the planting as it develops and adjusting it as necessary, the different plants will stay in proportion to each other and their pot. Cut back the shoots of a larger-leaved plant to a healthy-looking bud further down the stem if it starts to smother its smaller neighbours; careful pruning will maintain a balance between the two.

Some plants will need support. A cane pushed right through the root ball and as far into the compost as possible will prevent a top-heavy standard breaking in the wind. Tall species, like abutilons and standard fuchsias, can be tied to a

An improvised pot made from vine prunings, intertwined and lined with moss, makes a light and free-draining container.

cane with soft string, while some plants that would normally trail, such as *Helichrysum petiolare*, can be trained up a cane to produce an airy, tiered effect. You can also create an attractive feature by pushing willow stems around the edge of your container and tying them at the top to make a wigwam for climbing plants to use – clematis, jasmine and honeysuckle will happily oblige.

PROJECT: *BEYOND THE PAIL*

ALL SORTS OF HOUSEHOLD ITEMS can be adapted to make effective improvised containers. A zinc bucket, with holes drilled into the base for drainage, becomes a robust and stable pot for this tall planting of jasmine. Willow stems act as a support.

INGREDIENTS AND TOOLS
Zinc bucket
Electric drill
Gravel
Soil-based compost
Long willow shoots x 4
String
PLANTS
Jasminum polyanthum x 2

1 Gather together the materials and plants. Make sure the plants are well watered.

2 Turn the bucket upside down and drill a series of large drainage holes in the base.

3 Cover the bottom of the bucket with 3–5cm (1¼–2in) of gravel and part-fill with compost. Place the pots of jasmine in the bucket and adjust the level of the compost until the tops of the pots are just below the rim of the bucket. Take the plants out of their pots and place them in the bucket. Fill in with compost and water well.

4 Push the willow shoots into the compost around the bucket edge, following the angle of the sides of the bucket. This will splay out the shoots so that when they are tied together at the top they will be gracefully bowed. Loosely tie the jasmine shoots to the willow with string, so that the string will not cut into the young plants. Tie the willow stems together, with string, about 30cm (12in) from their tips. Other climbers, such as clematis and honeysuckle, could also be used for this project.

FAR RIGHT: *By cutting the willow stems when they are dormant and keeping the planting in a frost-free place, such as a sheltered doorway or conservatory, the willow shoots will root and become a living support for the jasmine.*

PROJECT: CONTAINER CONE

A LITTLE TIME AND EFFORT invested in making and planting this bulb cone in the autumn will pay dividends in spring, producing an exuberant mound of colour that will last for many weeks.

INGREDIENTS AND TOOLS
25cm (10in) diameter pot
60 x 90cm (2 x 3ft) of 2.5cm (1in) galvanized wire mesh
Wire cutters
Sphagnum moss
Soil-based compost

PLANTS
Muscari 'Blue Spire' x 100

1 Using the wire cutters, cut out a semi-circle, radius 45cm (18in), from the mesh.

2 Form the wire into a cone shape and tie the sides together by twisting the cut ends of the wire around themselves. Place the cone upside-down in the pot to hold it steady. Start lining the cone with

moss to a thickness of 2–3cm (¾–1¼in). Fill with approximately 5cm (2in) of compost. Arrange a circle of bulbs, almost touching, on the compost, each with its nose pushing down and outwards.

3 Work steadily up the cone in this way, adding moss, filling with compost, and placing a layer of bulbs every 4cm (1½in). Space the bulbs not more than 4cm (1½in) apart. Cover the filled cone with moss and secure it with a 'lid' of wire mesh.

4 Fill the pot with compost and invert the completed cone onto it. The top few centimetres of the cone are prone to drying out, so check regularly and water when necessary.

Pale pink scillas (above) and Muscari
'Blue Spire' (right) are ideal subjects
for this treatment, but do not be hesitant
about experimenting with other small
bulbs – dwarf narcissus or wood anemone,
in particular, would look very striking.

PROJECT: *Quirky Containers*

1 Assemble the plants and materials, ensuring the cistern has drainage holes. Add a layer of gravel followed by the compost. Plant the helictotrichon in the centre and surround it with the oxalis, plectranthus and begonias. Water well.

2 Saw the wire into lengths long enough to circle the heat exchanger twice, plus approximately 8cm (3in).

3 Bend a length of wire with pliers to form a short hook. Wrap the wire around the tube twice, then pull the end of the wire through the hook, bending it back

A TRIP TO A LOCAL SCRAPYARD produced two unusual objects for containers – an old copper cistern and a heat exchanger.

INGREDIENTS AND TOOLS
Copper cistern and heat exchanger
Gravel
Soil-based compost
Copper wire
Mini hacksaw and pliers
Plastic plant pot
PLANTS
Helictotrichon sempervirens x 1
Oxalis vulcanicola x 2
Plectranthus species x 2
Begonia rex cultivars x 3
Graptopetalum paraguayense x 2
Ceropegia woodii x 1

on itself. Repeat at intervals down the tube. Push a plastic plant pot halfway down the tube to act as a bung. Add compost to within 8–10cm (3–4in) of the top of the tube. Plant the remaining plants and firm in with compost.

RIGHT: *A modern, architectural garden is the perfect home for this striking display.*

PROJECT: *BATH TIME*

IN THIS WITTY SCHEME, a leaky hip bath is given a new lease of life as a surprisingly productive vegetable garden. Other large containers, such as enamel baby baths or old-fashioned sinks, are also suitable.

INGREDIENTS
Hip bath
Soil-based compost
Small terracotta pots x 20
Willow shoots x 4

PLANTS
Lettuce varieties, such as 'Red Salad Bowl', 'Little Gem' and 'Continuity', x 4 of each
Parsley x 2
Runner beans x 3

1 As the bath will be very heavy when filled with compost and plants, place it in its final position before you add the compost. Make sure there are sufficient drainage holes in the bottom.

2 Fill the bath with compost to within 4cm (1½in) of the rim. Arrange the pots upside-down in a pattern, to mark off the different planting sections.

3 Plant each lettuce variety in its own section and the parsley at the back.

4 Push in the willow shoots behind the parsley. Hoop one shoot across the others and tie to the upright shoots. Plant the beans at the base of the shoots.

LEFT AND ABOVE: *In time, the runner beans will cover the willow stems completely to transform the arrangement into an elegant garden sculpture, which would look as effective on a balcony as it would in a small yard. Pinching out the shoots regularly will keep the beans under control.*

PROJECT: *CORNER COLOUR*

CORNER CONTAINERS add interest to awkward areas around the house.

INGREDIENTS

Corner container, 90cm (3ft) in height
Soil-based compost
Slow-release fertilizer

PLANTS

Abutilon 'Ashford Red' x 1
Canna indica x 2
Mimulus aurantiacus x 2
Cuphea caeciliae x 2
Bidens ferulifolia x 3

1 Arrange the well-watered pots on the ground before planting. This makes it easier to see how you want to group them in the container. Obviously, large containers need large amounts of compost, and a false bottom helps to reduce the amount needed. A further saving can be made by rejuvenating last year's compost. Empty the compost into a wheelbarrow and add the required amount of slow-release fertilizer, following the manufacturer's instructions. Mix together thoroughly before returning to the container. Place the plants, still in their own pots, in the container and adjust the level of the compost until the top of the deepest pot is just below the rim of the container.

2 Remove the plants from their pots by supporting the stem and rootball with one hand and tapping the pot rim on a firm surface.

3 Place the abutilon and canna, which form the main structure of the planting, in the centre and at the back of the container. Place the mimulus, which will give an early focus of colour, at centre front, and the cuphea and bidens along the front; they will bush out and soften the edge of the container. Fill in with compost to within 5cm (2in) of the rim of the container and water well.

RIGHT: *The corner pot, with its rich and exotic scheme, is a dazzling focal point in a hitherto neglected part of the garden.*

THE LUXURIANT and cascading splendour of a well-planted hanging basket will enhance any garden. Hanging baskets offer the gardener great scope for inventiveness and imagination. As well as manufactured wire baskets, there are many unusual objects, such as coconut shells, buckets, colanders and vegetable baskets, that can be adapted to make effective containers. Although traditionally used to decorate doorways and porches, hanging baskets can play a more intimate role in the garden, suspended from an arbour or garden shed, or from the boughs of trees. Being imaginative with your choice and use of plants will result in more interesting displays, making hanging baskets objects of beauty in their own right.

Hanging Baskets

ABOVE: *A romantic, 'castles-in-the-air' effect can be created with a two-tier basket. This colour-themed arrangement uses both tender and hardy plants.*
LEFT: *A beautiful and abundant planting of* Begonia x tuberhybrida *'Diana Wynyard',* Helichrysum petiolare *and* Plectranthus coleoides *'Variegatus'.*

Types of Hanging Basket

Conventional hanging baskets vary from 30–50cm (12–20in) in diameter. The bigger the basket, the more voluptuous the effect, and plants will grow more vigorously and stay healthy longer in the extra compost. Flat-bottomed baskets are more stable for planting up, but they hold less compost.

You can replace the basket chains with coloured cord to tie in with the colours of the flowers or foliage, or with the paintwork of the house or garden furniture. Make sure the cord is strong enough to support the weight of the full basket, however, and will not rot if continually wet.

There is considerable scope for improvisation. A terracotta pot can be turned into a handsome hanging container by drilling three holes beneath the rim and using cord or rope to hang it. Car-boot sales and junk shops can also yield unusual 'baskets', from painted ceramic pots to birdcages.

Using Hanging Baskets

Baskets are usually hung by doorways, singly or in pairs, to soften the harsh lines of the architecture, and make an entrance more welcoming. They can be used to set off features such as arbours or pergolas, or to decorate less attractive garden

structures such as sheds. Quirky, improvised baskets, however, are more appropriate for enclosed, intimate spaces, where their eccentricity will not look out of place. For an unusual effect, hang baskets among the lower branches of trees where they will dangle like large, exotic fruits. Vary the heights of the baskets and use light-coloured plants – *Tolmiea menziesii* 'Taff's Gold', *Helichrysum petiolare* 'Limelight', tradescantias, chlorophytums, white petunias or busy Lizzies – which will appear to glow in the shade.

Although hanging baskets are ideal for trailing plants, you can use almost any plant to great effect – from argyranthemums and abutilons, through hostas and heucheras to zauschnerias. For a rich, flamboyant planting, mix colours in a basket; for elegance and sophistication, keep to a single-colour theme. Use plants with a graceful habit, dramatic leaf shape or distinctive flowers which look good from below – the double-flowered, pendulous *Begonia* x *hybrida* 'Pendula' combines all these qualities.

FOLIAGE SCHEMES

Foliage plays a crucial role in hanging basket displays, showing off flowers to maximum effect and giving substance to a planting. Large-leaved plants, such as *Hedera colchica* or *Pelargonium* 'Chocolate Peppermint', will add weight and stature to arrangements. Use grasses like *Molinia caerulea* 'Variegata' and *Felicia petiolata* to arch out over them.

To create a lighter look, you can use trailers with cut leaves or paler foliage: *Pelargonium* 'Atomic Snowflake', for example, or *Helichrysum petiolare*, *Anthemis punctata cupaniana*, *Senecio*

ABOVE: **Simple displays require simple backdrops. Bare woodwork gives these pelargoniums and their curved wire basket a chance to stand out.**
FAR LEFT: **Curled wire hooked onto zinc buckets adds a quirky touch to this improvised display.**

leucostachys or *Bidens ferulifolia*. *Rhodochiton atrosanguineus* will twine its way up the chains of the basket to show off its dusky flowers, while *Tropaeolum peregrinum* used in the same way will produce a brighter and more cheerful effect.

WINTER INTEREST

Although flower colour is in short supply during the winter, there is no reason to neglect your baskets. There are plenty of attractive evergreen plants that are able to withstand cold weather. Use ivy with varieties of *Vinca major* or *V. minor*

to trail gracefully and provide movement. Contrast the silvery *Cerastium tomentosum* with the dark green fingers of *Helleborous foetidus* and the leathery leaves of *Bergenia purpurea* to create a rich texture.

On their own, winter-flowering pansies can look bedraggled, but mixing them with evergreen foliage or the colourful shoots of cornus or willow will lift the display. A jumble of different-coloured pansies can look untidy in the bleak winter garden, so use pure, single colours, if possible.

Other good choices for winter are: *Euonymus* 'Silver Queen', with variegated foliage, *Euphorbia myrsinites*, with trailing stems of glaucous foliage, *Festuca glauca*, an upright blue grass, *Ophiopogon planiscapus* 'Nigrescens', a black grass, and *Iberis sempervirens*, with small, evergreen leaves and white, scented flowers in spring.

PREPARATION AND MAINTENANCE

A well-planted hanging basket should be entirely smothered by flowers and foliage within a few weeks – and should stay that way. So it is well worth taking the time and making the effort to prepare and look after a basket properly.

BASKET LINERS

A good basket liner should allow air and water to penetrate, to keep the roots of the plants healthy. It should be easy to cut, enabling you to make planting holes where you choose. If you are using a liner with pre-cut holes, the holes should be able to accommodate plants of different sizes.

Hardy pansies, ivy and lamiums will give a colourful display over a long season.

Sphagnum moss is the material traditionally used to line hanging baskets. However, although it meets all the practical requirements and looks attractive, increasing concerns about the exploitation of peat reserves have seen it supplanted in recent years by more environmentally friendly materials. One such example is coir matting. Neat and durable, it can be shaped to fit any size of basket; to plant through the matting, simply cut holes with a pair of scissors. Wool fibre is another option. These natural linings should be discarded after about a year (they will readily degrade on the compost heap). Pre-formed rigid fibre liners last longer but are more limiting in terms of plant positioning, while the black plastic varieties inevitably show through a planting.

ABOVE: *A bizzare-looking mix of echeverias and* **Agave americana 'Variegata'** *proves that there are really no limits to what you can grow in a basket.*
ABOVE LEFT: *With their healthy and vigorous growth, these petunias and brachycomes will soon disguise the basket liner.*

COMPOST

Soil-based composts (see pages 15–16) are the best choice for hanging baskets as they give up their water reserve slowly. However, a large basket containing soil-based compost will be extremely heavy, so use equal amounts of peat- and soil-based composts to make a lighter mixture. Water-retentive gels (see page 17) will help maintain a good water supply.

FIXING THE BASKET

All hanging baskets must be securely fixed. For wall-hung baskets, drill and plug the wall, then screw in strong brackets. Holding an empty basket against the wall first will help you to gauge the correct position; the basket should be high enough to allow you to pass by without getting a faceful of wet foliage. The plants may grow approximately 23cm (9in) out from the basket, so take this into account, too.

If the basket is to hang from a pergola or beam, either hook it to a rope tied around the wood, or screw a heavy hook into the wood and hang the basket from there.

To prevent a wall-hung basket from blowing around in the wind, push two thin canes horizontally into the body of the basket at the back. By forming a triangle with the wall as they rest against it, the canes act as an efficient brace.

PLANTING UP

Remove the chains, if possible, and sit the basket in a large flowerpot, or hang it at a workable height; though awkward, this method enables you to see how the display is developing as you plant.

Put a layer of moss or wool fibre in the bottom and lay a piece of plastic sheet across it, dishing it slightly so that it will retain some moisture. For rigid fibre or plastic liners, which are fairly moisture-retentive, you can omit the sheet. If you are using coir matting, overlap the pieces so that no gaps are left, and trim any surplus from around the top, before adding the sheet. You can either cut planting holes at this stage, before adding the compost, or make them one at a time as you plant your way up the basket.

Add the compost and start planting near the bottom of the basket with some plants that will spread widthways, others that will trail and give depth. Lobelias are good, reliable plants for in-filling. If you are using bedding plants, buy them in single rather than mixed colours, so that you will have more control over the colour scheme.

Plant at regular intervals as you work your way around and up the basket and use a good mix of plant types. Start to introduce larger plants from halfway up. Do not plant right to the top of the sides as water tends to run out of the plant holes near the rim without penetrating the compost; growth from the top will soon hide the baldness.

At the top, start around the edge, angling plants to encourage their foliage to cover the rim. Work inwards, creating variety and contrasts by mixing foliage and trailing plants. Large baskets can sustain some larger plants, but will need plenty of water; make a dip in the compost's surface as you finish planting to help the water soak in.

WATERING

Do not water the basket until it has been hung but thereafter remember to water frequently and regularly. To avoid having to climb onto chairs or up ladders with a watering can, either attach a hose to a broom handle, or use a lightweight, hand-held pump that pumps water up a hooked pipe and into the basket. There are compact pulley systems on the market that raise and lower the basket for you to water and deadhead.

With careful combinations of textures, colours and forms, a richly planted basket becomes a garden in its own right.

PROJECT: *BACK TO NATURE*

MADE ENTIRELY from natural products, this hanging basket has a very rustic character. Once past its prime, it can be consigned to the compost heap where every part of it will eventually break down to return its goodness to the soil.

INGREDIENTS

25cm (10in) diameter wicker basket
Woollen fleece liner
Soil-based compost
Stout clematis stems x 2
String

PLANTS

White petunias x 3
Nemesia fruticans x 3
Silene uniflora 'Flore Pleno' x 3
Polygonum capitatum x 3

1 Assemble the plants and materials. Make sure the plants are well watered.

2 Line the basket with a thin, even layer of woollen fleece.

3 Fill the basket two-thirds full of compost, firming it down onto the fleece.

4 Position the petunias and nemesia in the middle of the basket with the silene and polygonum trailing over the sides. Carefully feed compost around the plants, firming in gently. Water well. Bend one end of a clematis stem around a handle and tie with string. Tie the other end to the opposite handle. Repeat with the second stem of clematis and the two remaining handles.

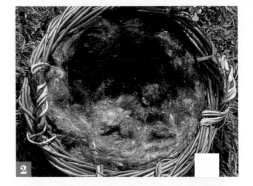

RIGHT: *Hanging from the branch of a tree, the basket is in perfect harmony with its surroundings, highlighted against a backdrop of green foliage.*

PROJECT: *FEAST OF FOLIAGE*

FOLIAGE OF DIFFERENT textures and tones with just a few flowers as highlights makes a stunning display.

INGREDIENTS AND TOOLS

45cm (18in) diameter wire basket

Large plastic pot

Plastic carrier bag

Scissors

Sphagnum moss

Soilless compost

PLANTS

Pelargonium 'Atomic Snowflake' x 1

Pelargonium 'Decora Rose' x 2

Helichrysum petiolare x 2

Petunia 'Pink Chiffon' x 4

Plectranthus coleoides 'Variegatus' x 2

Silver-leaved *Begonia rex* x 1

Large-leaved begonia x 1

Purple-leaved *Begonia rex* x 1

1 Remove the chains from the basket and stand on the pot for stability. Cut a circle 25cm (10in) in diameter from the bag.

2 Line the bottom third of the basket with a layer of moss 2–3cm (¾–1¼in) thick. Place the circle on the moss and cover with compost to just below the level of the moss. Press down firmly. Gently squeeze the rootballs of the trailing pelargoniums and helichrysum, then ease them through the wires or feed the foliage through from inside the basket.

3 Work up the basket, alternately lining with moss and filling with compost. Insert the remaining plants at irregular intervals, using the begonia leaves as a central focus. Stand back regularly to check the balance of the planting.

RIGHT: *In sun or dappled shade, this rich, leafy planting adds sophistication to a cottage garden setting.*

TYPES OF WINDOWBOX

Windowboxes are available in a range of materials – natural and man-made – and a variety of sizes to fit most sills. Buy the largest box your sill can take, as an undersized box can look lost. A narrow sill, or no sill at all, does not mean you cannot have a box; support it on brackets instead.

As with baskets and pots, you can improvise windowboxes from old household items. Empty food tins make cheap alternatives to manufactured boxes; wire them together for extra stability and give them a coat of paint or varnish inside and out if you want them to last more than a year.

TERRACOTTA AND STONE

Terracotta is one of the most popular materials used for windowboxes – it looks good in any location, can be decorated in a number of ways, and suits both formal or informal plantings. The weight of a terracotta box makes it quite stable but if there is any danger of it being dislodged, drill small holes at the back or sides and fix it with wires or nylon to hooks or vine eyes in the wall.

If the box is to be a year-round feature, make sure that the terracotta is frostproof. Terracotta also dries out rapidly, so you will need to water frequently – more so in hot or windy weather.

Stone and concrete troughs are too heavy to be used on sills but can be placed on the ground or raised on improvised plinths of weathered brick, stone or wood under ground-floor windows. Stark and bright when new, they weather with age to more attractive, mellow tones.

PLASTIC

Plastic windowboxes are inexpensive and easy to move around. Although quite unobtrusive, they are not usually very attractive, but you can hide the dark brown and green versions quite easily by using trailing plants. Avoid white plastic, however, as this will show through even the most luxuriant of plantings. Used inside larger wooden or terracotta windowboxes, plastic boxes make excellent water-retentive liners.

WOOD

Wooden windowboxes are easy to make, which is a boon if you cannot find a ready-made one to fit the sill. Inserting a rigid plastic liner will help

Terracotta replicas of lead windowboxes are durable and relatively lightweight. This planting is deliberately kept simple so as not to detract from the decorative detailing on the box.

plain box, but will give a planting more interest as trailers begin to creep through them. Alternatively, nail thin dowel or rope onto the wood in a variety of patterns, or staple attractive mahonia or holly leaves or lengths of colourful willow or dogwood stems to the box. These will give a bright, rustic look that is particularly effective with winter plantings.

METAL

Galvanized boxes and wrought-iron and wire baskets make good, sturdy and durable windowboxes. Untreated metal will need to be painted to prevent rusting, or given a coat of varnish. Galvanized tin, however, is already rust-proof and can be left untreated. It may look glaringly bright at first but its shiny surface will gradually oxidize to an attractive soft grey.

ABOVE: *A galvanized windowbox with a simple spring display of hyacinths and variegated ivy.*
RIGHT: *A plain stone trough is the perfect foil for this lush planting of begonias, pelargoniums, trailing ivy and plectranthus.*

keep the interior of the box dry, thereby extending its life. In addition, wooden windowboxes look appealing in almost any setting, whether traditional or modern, and can be made to look rustic or sophisticated with different surface treatments, such as varnish, stain or paint.

Wooden boxes can be decorated in various ways. Use an electric jigsaw to cut a decorative edge or a series of ornamental holes in the sides. Making holes not only improves the look of a

Using Windowboxes

Despite their name, windowboxes can be used in almost any setting – as freestanding troughs on a patio, for instance, or as decorative details, alternated with flowerpots, to outline a roof terrace. They also make good wall or shelf planters; fixed securely in staggered rows above one another, they can add colourful interest to a bare expanse of wall in a courtyard.

Planting Schemes

A successful windowbox planting has to fulfil a number of criteria: it needs to be in harmony with its immediate surroundings and to have a structure that is strong enough to remain in good shape for several months. Cascades of colour in the form of trailing fuchsias, ivy-leaved pelargoniums and pendulous begonias will transform the exterior of a house, but the display must look good from inside as well. Bear in mind that plants in windowboxes tend to lean away from the

ABOVE: *This windowbox displays a sensitive use of colour, despite containing many different plants, including diascias, bacopas and petunias.*
ABOVE LEFT: *An abundance of herbs is as visually appealing as it is useful.*

window towards the light. Furthermore, for most of the day, incoming sunlight means the plants will be visible only in silhouette. By using plants with a strong architectural quality, such as cordylines, you can create bold shapes that will look striking whatever the time of day.

A windowbox can be planted specifically to complement a trough positioned below a ground-floor window. The two plantings do not have to be identical; they will look attractive if they merely echo each other while retaining their distinct characters. Using vertical forms such as *Anisodontea capensis* below and trailing forms such as *Convolvulus sabatius* above will encourage the plantings to grow into one another.

If you have no garden, a sunny windowsill is the ideal place to grow a few herbs. A small boxful is as decorative as it is practical; the widely varied leaf shapes and textures of parsley, marjoram, thyme, chives, oregano, nasturtiums, basil and sage create attractive foliage combinations, and their sweet aromas will fill the air.

Fragrant plants are particularly important in windowbox plantings. The unmistakable scent of hyacinths and wallflowers in the spring, and allysums, *Verbena* 'Loveliness' and stocks in the summer will be even more intoxicating carried in directly from a windowbox rather than diluted in an open garden.

As a windowbox planting is a decorative feature of your property, it should always complement its architecture. A formal townhouse with tall windows lends itself to a smart, formal planting, while a less restrained planting using a wider variety of shapes and textures would be more suitable for an informal location, such as an old-fashioned cottage with windows of different sizes and shapes.

Although often hard to place, purple petunias combine well with helichrysum, verbena and lobelia. Each complements the other, as well as the house, to produce a stunning effect.

A cheerful windowbox display of white and yellow daffodils with trailing ivies provides welcome colour in early spring.

The more formal the situation, the greater the need for symmetry in a windowbox planting. A dramatic, ordered arrangement of strong shapes makes a real impact against a large, imposing window, whereas a more informal planting of delicately coloured flowers would simply be overshadowed.

An informal planting can be structured so that it appears to defy the space restrictions of the windowbox. By combining plants that arch and spread with upright and trailing varieties, you can build up a multi-layered mass of flowers and foliage tumbling and billowing out of the box.

SEASONAL PLANTING

Permanent year-round structure can be provided by evergreens such as box, euonymus, hebes and ivies. The effect can be changed each season by introducing bulbs, perennials and annuals in succession. It is best to sink seasonal plants into the box in their individual pots, as moving plants in and out can disturb the permanent inhabitants.

Plants in a winter windowbox are exposed to severe conditions. If sheltered by an overhanging ledge, they are likely to get very dry; prolonged frosts create difficult growing conditions and strong winds can be damaging as they strike the façade of a building with considerable force.

Tough evergreen plants with different leaf shapes and different textures will make an interesting winter display that lasts: *Polypodium vulgare*, *Epimedium pinnatum*, *Iris foetidissima*, *Bergenia* 'Abendglut', *Euphorbia myrsinites* and *Hebe albicans* 'Red Edge' are all ideal candidates. Underplanting with snowdrops and winter aconites will give you some colour early in the year, while smaller varieties of daffodils – *Narcissus triandus*, *N.* 'W.P. Milner' and *N. poeticus*, for example – will prolong the interest until the summer planting is due.

Mixed annuals like nemesias, candytuft, larkspur and lobelias have a simplicity and charm, while free-flowering plants like bidens and felicia produce an airy effect. All of these plants would make ideal choices for a colourful and vivacious cottage windowbox in summer.

PREPARATION AND MAINTENANCE

Whether you have a single windowbox or a number that form part of a grander planting scheme, good preparation is always worthwhile. With a little care you can grow strong, healthy plants that will form long-lasting displays requiring relatively little maintenance.

COMPOST AND DRAINAGE

Windowboxes dry out rapidly, so use soil-based compost, which retains water well (see page 15). Its weight will also help keep boxes stable.

Good drainage is essential. Make sure there are plenty of holes in the bottom of the box and check occasionally to ensure they have not been blocked by packed compost or roots; clear them from below with a stick, if necessary. If the box is raised, place 5cm (2in) of gravel in the bottom to act as a sump until the excess water drains away.

Check boxes regularly. It is easy to assume that a windowbox gets watered every time it rains, when, in fact, no water may reach it at all, if it is sheltered by an overhang, for example, or if the wind blows the rain in the opposite direction.

An upstairs windowbox should be placed on a tray so that you can water it without splashing passers-by below. Raising the box on small blocks will prevent it becoming waterlogged.

Raising this water trough off the ground and drilling drainage holes provides a free-draining container for **Anthemis punctata cupaniana.**

POSITIONING AND FIXING

A windowsill may be the most obvious place to site a windowbox, but it may not be the most practical if the sill slopes, or if the windows open outwards. Securing the box on brackets is a good solution. When you come to position the brackets, remember that you will need to be able to reach the box easily to water, weed, deadhead and prune. It is also better as well to plant the box *in situ* through an open window, rather than struggling up a ladder laden with a planted box.

It is essential to use strong, well-secured fittings to support the windowbox. Bolting or screwing the box to these is another safety measure worth taking. Attach brackets to the wall using wall plugs and brass or zinc screws that will not corrode, but get advice from a professional builder before you drill into rendered walls.

PROJECT: *SHELF LIFE*

1 Assemble the plants and materials. Cut out a cardboard circle slightly smaller than the outside diameter of the top of the pot. Paint the brackets and the wood.

2 Draw a central line along the length and width of the piece of wood. Using these two lines to guide you, centre the cardboard template and draw a circle. Mark out four more, evenly spaced circles.

3 Drill through the board, just touching the inside of one circle. Insert the jigsaw blade into the hole and saw around the circle. Repeat for the four other circles. Screw the brackets onto the shelf at convenient points and hold the shelf in position on the wall, using a spirit level to ensure it is horizontal. Mark the position of the screw holes on the wall and remove the shelf. With a masonry bit, drill the holes in the wall. Tap in the plugs, replace the shelf and screw it to the wall. Add compost to the pots and plant the pelargoniums. Place the pots in the holes.

THIS SHELF gives you the flexibility to change the plants as often as you like, to create new schemes or simply replace the odd plant that is past its best.

INGREDIENTS AND TOOLS

15cm (6in) diameter clay pots x 5
Cardboard
Treated wood, measuring 25 x 90 x 2.5cm
    (10 x 36 x 1in)
Brackets x 2
External wood paint and paintbrush
Pencil
Electric drill and jigsaw
4cm (1½in) screws and plugs
Spirit level
Soilless compost
PLANTS
Pelargonium 'Eclipse Red' x 5

RIGHT: *This simple shelf is an attractive alternative to a windowbox where there is no windowsill, and allows you to see the wonderful patina that has built up on the clay pots.*

PROJECT: WOODLAND TROUGH

1 Cut the stems into 20cm (8in) lengths. Mark two parallel lines along the box, about 4cm (1½in) in from either edge. Using the lines as guides, fix stems of an even thickness to the box with the hammer and staples. Stagger the staples to ensure closer coverage. Staple longer, pliable stems across the front of the box to form patterns.

2 Spread a layer of gravel in the box for drainage. Then fill the box with compost.

3 Place the iris in the centre of the box, with the ferns and hellebores symmetrically to either side, and intersperse with snowdrops. Firm in with more compost and water well.

RIGHT: *This evergreen planting will be effective throughout the year, with seasonal highlights of white snowdrops and scarlet iris seed pods.*

STAPLING TWIGS ONTO a wooden box or trough creates a colourful and rustic container for a woodland-style planting.

INGREDIENTS AND TOOLS
Treated wooden box, measuring
   110 x 20 x 20cm (43 x 8 x 8in)
Willow stems (*Salix daphnoides*,
   S. alba 'Vitellina' and 'Britzensis')
Secateurs
1cm (½in) galvanized staples
Hammer
Coarse gravel
Soilless compost
PLANTS
Iris foetidissima x 1
Asplenium scolopendrium cristatum x 2
Polypodium vulgare x 2
Helleborus foetidus x 2
Galanthus nivalis x 20

SHRUBS AND CLIMBERS

ABUTILON

Producing maple-like leaves and showy, pendent, bell-shaped flowers, abutilons are strong-growing, reaching 2–3m (6½–10ft) in height. Plants can be kept smaller by cutting back hard annually or taking cuttings in summer to produce new plants. With their robust upright growth, they are good for forming the framework of a planting; the large leaves add strength to architectural arrangements and give structure to frothier plantings. 'Boule de Neige' has white flowers, 'Canary Bird' soft yellow and 'Nabob' deep red. *A. pictum* 'Thompsonii' has delicate-looking, yellow mottled leaves and orange flowers.

ARTEMISIA 'POWIS CASTLE'

This small evergreen shrub, 90cm (3ft) high, with finely cut, silver-grey foliage, looks good with yellows and purple, and against broad or strap-like leaves. It gives a hot, dry effect and combines well with purple sage (*Salvia officinalis* 'Purpurascens') and *Penstemon* 'Alice Hindley'. Tolerant of drastic pruning, it can be kept small.

CUPHEA (CIGAR FLOWER)

Cuphea species bring subtle touches of orange to planting schemes. *C. ignea* is a fresh green plant that produces orange-red tubular blooms, each with a white rim, non-stop throughout the summer. The variegated form has yellow mottled leaves, which show up well in dappled light. Both grow to 60cm (2ft) in height. *C. caeciliae* is

The delicate orange flowers of **Cuphea caeciliae** *add warmth to an arrangement of argyranthemums and mimulus.*

vigorous and bushy with orange and red flowers on red stems and is a good provider of dark green foliage for backing orange or red schemes.

FUCHSIA

Fuchsia flowers range from the sublime to the ridiculous, from overblown, many-petalled monsters to the most exquisite soft orange, green-tipped tubular blooms. 'Red Spider' is a graceful, half-hardy hanging basket plant, trailing 45–60cm (18–24in), whose uncomplicated red flowers with long narrow sepals and shorter petals produce a rich effect. In complete contrast, the tender 'Thalia' is an upright grower 60–90cm (2–3ft) high, and a star in its own right with dramatic dark red-green, downy foliage. Flowers are long narrow red tubes held in clusters at the end of the shoots. *F. magellanica* 'Versicolor' has leaves of pink, grey, white and green that create a symphony of colour with the fine pendulous drops of its deep red flowers, and its effect cannot be overstated. It is ideal for large containers, reaching a height of 75cm (2½ft) and spread of 90cm (3ft). 'Marinka' is a half-hardy trailing variety with dark green leaves and dark red flowers that makes a solid base planting for a hanging basket. 'Golden Marinka' is its variegated form. Low-growing, to 10cm (4in), and half-hardy, *F. procumbens* is very unfuchsia-like, with curious upright flowers of yellow, brown, green and blue, and large shiny fruits. Tender *F. fulgens* has soft orange, tubular flowers with green-tipped sepals and large, pale green leaves. The young foliage has a frosted appearance. It can grow to 1.8m (6ft), though it usually stays smaller in a container, and is well suited to large displays and backyard-jungle effects.

LAVATERA MARITIMA

Like a more subtle version of an hibiscus, *L. maritima* has large, lilac trumpet flowers with a dark centre and soft sage-green foliage. It will grow to a height of 1.5m (5ft), but can be kept within bounds by cutting back hard. Use it with pinks like

Osteospermum 'Pink Whirls' or contrast it with bold foliage and dark flowers, such as *Cosmos atrosanguineus* and *Sedum telephium maximum* 'Atropurpureum'.

LOTUS HIRSUTUS
A delightful small shrub, 25–60cm (10–24in) high, with softly hairy, small silver-grey leaves. The tight heads of its pea-like flowers are small and white with a subtle pink tinge, and are followed in autumn by conspicuous shiny red-brown seed pods. Try it with other 'woolies' such as *Stachys citrina* or *Lagurus ovatus*, the furry hare's-tail grass.

PLEIOBLASTUS AURICOMUS
Although many bamboos are extremely tall, vigorous plants, they can be grown successfully in containers, provided they are given good conditions. They enjoy a rich compost that is kept moist but not necessarily wet. Less vigorous than many, *P. auricomus* can be cut back each spring and, if fed well, makes a thicket of shoots 90cm (3ft) high. Its yellow and green striped leaves brighten shady corners, though it is equally happy in full sun.

SOLANUM
Related to the potato, these plants make vigorous growers for large containers. *S. jasminoides* is potentially a very large climber, 5m (16ft) and taller, but young plants from cuttings are more likely to make 1.8–2.5m (6–8ft). It produces clusters of small, pale blue flowers which are particularly effective when allowed to

scramble through a planting and out of the pot. 'Album' is the delightful white form. *S. laciniatum* deserves a large pot on its own. It is a robust plant, 1.2–1.5m (4–5ft) high, with very deeply cut leaves and blue flowers, followed by orange seed pods which hang like small eggs. It is easily grown from seed or cuttings. Vigorous and cheerful, *S. rantonnetii* is a bright green bush, 1.5m (5ft) high, bearing blue flowers with a yellow eye. Try it with *Osteospermum ecklonis* 'Blue Streak' or the large-leaved hedychiums.

PERENNIALS

AGAPANTHUS
These classic container plants, growing 90cm (3ft) high, make an impressive sight with their broad, strap-like leaves and great umbels of flowers. There are many named varieties, giving a range of flower colours from the rich deep blue of *A.* 'Midnight Blue' through the mid-blue of *A.* 'Headbourne Hybrids' to *A.* 'Bressingham White'. Use the darkest blues with clear yellow flowers such as *Argyranthemum* 'Jamaica Primrose' or *Coreopsis verticillata* 'Moonbeam'.

ANTHEMIS PUNCTATA CUPANIANA
A vigorous, mat-forming perennial, 30cm (12in) high, with white, yellow-eyed daisies that grow on short stems over the finely cut, silvery foliage. Its vigour may overwhelm lesser plants but, despite this, it has an elegant appearance, and can be cut back hard if necessary. Use it to trail

over the side of a pot or from a hanging basket, where, combined with pink argyranthemums or tangled with *Convolvulus althaeoides*, it will create a light, romantic effect. For a contrast, grow it with *Tradescantia zebrina*.

ARGYRANTHEMUM (MARGUERITE)
The epitome of a summer container plant. Clouds of flowers are produced right through the season on this bushy evergreen woody perennial with fresh green, deeply cut leaves. Argyranthemums are easy to propagate, fast growing (reaching 90cm/3ft) and will soon fill a large container. They also make impressive standards. Shear off the fading heads to encourage new flower buds. 'Jamaica Primrose' is a vigorous plant with wonderful large, clear yellow, daisy flowers. 'Vancouver' has double pink flowers which develop a large central boss, while *A. gracile* 'Chelsea Girl' has white daisy flowers over fine, thread-like, grey-green leaves. On their own they create a misty romantic effect, but give still greater impact if used with bold foliage. Try a mixed planting with *Osteospermum* 'Whirlygig', *Phormium tenax* 'Purpureum' and *Verbena bonariensis*.

ARUM ITALICUM 'PICTUM'
Rich green, spear-shaped leaves, boldly marbled with grey or pale green, make this one of the most exciting herbaceous plants for winter effect. The leaves appear in autumn, reaching a height and spread of 30cm (12in), and die away in spring. Plants will need some shelter from

strong winds. Combine with *Bergenia purpurascens* or the holly-like leaves of *Osmanthus heterophyllus*.

BEGONIA

This is a genus that embraces extravagantly flowered plants, such as the tuberous varieties of begonia with their enormous double flowers, as well as some of the most subtle and delectable of foliage plants. In crowded, still conditions a few begonias can be susceptible to mildew, but this is easily controlled with an occasional spray of fungicide. *B. semperflorens* has flowers in red, white and pink, and leaves in green or shiny bronze. The plants are compact, 30cm (12in) high, with fleshy stems and leaves, and are ideal for interplanting in hanging baskets and windowboxes to give an early mature look.

B. rex hybrids have large, characteristically begonia-shaped leaves patterned with pink and purple, many with silver speckling. They range in height from 20–40cm (8–16in). *B. sutherlandii* has dainty clusters of soft orange flowers which look especially good with the foliage of *Helichrysum petiolare* 'Limelight'. It dies back in winter and can be propagated from tubers produced on the stems. Grown in pots, it will make a trailing mound up to 30–60cm (1–2ft) high and wide. The *B.* x *tuberhybrida* Pendula Group are robust plants, 45–60cm (1½–2ft) tall, which hang well from baskets. Choose the slightly double varieties in yellow or white and hang in baskets where they will be back-lit by the morning or evening sun

Begonias in soft pastel colours are ideal for lightening shady areas of the garden.

to make the planting glow. *B. fuchsioides* is an upright plant, 60–120cm (2–4ft) high, with small, serrated, glossy leaves and small red flowers produced almost continuously. Its strong, reddish-coloured stems give a good vertical line, so use it as the central plant in a group and contrast it with larger, softer leaves.

BIDENS FERULIFOLIA

A feathery plant that reaches a height and spread of 60–90cm (2–3ft), *B. ferulifolia* produces warm yellow flowers on thin stems. Its wind tolerance makes it a useful trailer for hanging baskets where it will scramble amongst other plants, putting up its bright flowers here and there. It is easily rooted from cuttings. Use it with yellow or red cannas and crocosmias.

CONVOLVULUS

Relatives of the invasive bindweed, convolvulus make colourful sun-loving scramblers when confined to a pot. The hardy *C. althaeoides* has finely cut leaves of silvery green, long trailing stems and large pink trumpet flowers that open in the sun. It grows to 60–90cm (2–3ft) and can be planted to trail or to climb up a support; stand pots on a hard surface to prevent the vigorous roots establishing themselves in the ground and putting up new shoots. Low-growing and non-invasive, *C. sabatius* has cheerful, blue-purple flowers throughout the summer and small, fresh green leaves on trailing stems 15–20cm (6–8in) long. It is tolerant of a degree or two of frost.

COREOPSIS VERTICILLATA 'MOONBEAM'

Delicate, primrose-yellow daisy flowers
are combined with dark hair-like foliage on
a distinctive plant, 45–60cm (1½–2ft) tall,
that looks equally good growing alone or
combined with the grassy leaves of *Molinia
caerulea* 'Variegata'.

COSMOS ATROSANGUINEUS

This is a very striking plant which
produces maroon flowers on long stalks
late in the season and grows to a height of
45cm (18in). For winter protection, lift the
tuberous root and store it in a frost-free
place, as you would a dahlia. The flowers
have the scent of cocoa and are sometimes
so dark they appear as intriguing little
black holes, an effect which can add
interest to a pedestrian planting. Good
as a partner for *Argyranthemum gracile*
'Chelsea Girl'.

CROCOSMIA

Not an obvious choice for containers,
but, given the shortage of orange-, red-
and yellow-flowered plants with distinctive
foliage, crocosmias are often very useful.
The flower spikes appear late in the
summer but the upright, sword-shaped
leaves make a good impression throughout
the season. The variety 'Lucifer' is 90cm
(3ft) tall, with intense red flowers.
'Citronella' has golden-yellow flowers,
and 'Solfaterre' pale apricot-yellow, with
attractive, dusky bronze foliage. Both grow
to 45–75cm (1½–2½ft) in height. Grow
with cannas or hedychiums to create a
jungle-like effect.

DAHLIA

The continued hybridizing of dahlias has
led to an almost infinite range of sizes
and colours. The dwarf varieties, at 30cm
(12in) high, are easier to manage in a pot
than the large border types, but lack their
stature and presence. Grow the tall
varieties in large pots for a dashing and
colourful display on a grand scale. They
need plenty of water so are best grown
without competition from other plants.
Place them out of strong winds and
overwinter the tubers in a frost-free place.
'Bishop of Llandaff', with its exceptional
purple foliage and intense red flowers,
grows to 90cm (3ft) high. Plant it with
white cosmos, *Argyranthemum gracile*
'Chelsea Girl' or, for an intense red
arrangement, with *Canna* 'America'.

DIASCIA

A greater number of diascia hybrids are
now becoming available. All are free-
flowering, and elegant shades of pink.
D. vigilis is a pretty, gentle plant with
spikes of flowers on dainty, airy stems
and leaves of soft fresh green. *D. rigescens*
has distinctive coppery-pink flowers and,
with its tough, toothed leaves, is more
rugged-looking. Both grow to a height of
30–45cm (12–18in). *D.* 'Lilac Belle' is a
small-flowered, more compact variety,
23cm (9in) high.

EUCOMIS BICOLOR

This is a solid-looking plant, consisting of a
substantial rosette of broad, wavy-edged
leaves from which rises a dense spike of
pale green flowers topped, pineapple-like,

by a rosette of bracts. Reaching an
eventual height of 45cm (18in), it looks
best when contrasted with lighter and
wispier subjects.

FELICIA

These are evergreen perennials with
daisy-like flowers. From late spring to
autumn, *F. amelloides* carries an abundance
of yellow-eyed, sky-blue flowers on long
stalks above the foliage. The small foliage
itself makes little impact, so deadhead by
shearing to encourage more flowers. Plants
grow to a height of 30cm (12in). *F.a.* 'Santa
Anita' has larger flowers on a more robust-
looking plant. 'Reads White' is the white
variety. *F. petiolata* is a very different plant
and much hardier, withstanding several
degrees of frost. It has soft grey-green
leaves on stems that arch out, and small
pink flowers. Mix it in with stronger foliage
and use it in hanging baskets and to trail
out of boxes and pots.

FESTUCA GLAUCA

A useful small, clump-forming grass,
10cm (4in) high, with stiff, intense blue-
grey leaves. Divide a clump and put small
sections among other plants to 'spike up'
the textural quality of an arrangement.
Try juxtaposing it with the purple fleshy
leaves of *Sedum* 'Bertram Anderson'.

GAZANIA

These gay, sun-loving plants, 20cm (8in)
high, have large, daisy-like flowers in
brilliant shades of red, orange and yellow,
which open in the sun. The foliage may be

grey or green. Though perennials, they are usually grown as seed-raised annuals, but named varieties can be propagated from cuttings in late summer. 'Cream Beauty' is a more subdued colour than most and has grey-green, downy leaves. It is useful on its own or with strong, clear blue flowers such as those of *Convolvulus sabatius*.

HAKONECHLOA MACRA 'AUREOLA'
This very bright green and yellow striped grass, making a dense clump of arching leaves 30cm (12in) high, adds lightness and grace to a planting. It associates well with a range of colours including white petunias, acid yellow *Coreopsis verticillata* 'Moonbeam', soft yellow *Argyranthemum* 'Jamaica Primrose', apricot *Mimulus aurantiacus* and *Lobelia* 'Lilac Cascade'. Use it as a main plant with other, smaller plants to cover the rim of the planter.

HEDYCHIUM (GINGER LILY)
These are impressive foliage plants with exciting showy flowers, good for bold foliage arrangements and for creating a jungle-like effect. *H. gardnerianum*, 1.5–2m (5–6½ft) tall, produces spikes of soft yellow and red flowers in late summer. *H. densiflorum*, a smaller variety at 90–150cm (3–5ft), has ribbed foliage and soft orange flowers in dense spikes.

HELICHRYSUM PETIOLARE
This is one of the top ten plants for containers, providing a firm but graceful base to a planting. It has trailing stems, sweeping out horizontally, and small,

heart-shaped, grey, felted leaves that look good in any colour scheme. 'Limelight' is particularly effective with soft clear oranges, for example, *Begonia sutherlandii* and the pale forms of *Mimulus aurantiacus*. The heads of the creamy yellow flowers on long stalks can be a distraction, so cut them off, if you prefer, and prune the whole plant occasionally to stop it swamping smaller displays.

HELICTOTRICHON SEMPERVIRENS
This dense clump of blue-grey upright leaves, 60–90cm (2–3ft) high, makes a useful evergreen feature plant for a large container. Try it with pink *Argyranthemum foeniculaceum*, which complements its narrow foliage, or with the felted leaves of *Helichrysum petiolare*.

HOSTA
These handsome, clump-forming plants, producing flowers of lilac or white on upright stems, positively thrive when grown in pots. Leaves vary from the very large, 30cm (12in) across in *H. sieboldiana*, to only 2.5–5cm (1–2in) in *H. venusta*. Many forms have bold variegation and some make a bright show of yellow as the leaves die back in the autumn.
H. var *albopicta* is 60cm (2ft) high, with young leaves of bright yellow and green that colour briefly in autumn to orangey yellow. *H.* 'Krossa Regal' is a large plant with a height of 45cm (1½ft) and spread of 75cm (2½ft), blue-green leaves and tall spikes of lilac flowers. *H. lancifolia*, with shiny, dark green, narrow, pointed leaves, gives a lighter, more grassy effect than the

larger-leaved types. Perhaps the ultimate in large hostas, *H. sieboldiana* var. *elegans* has rounded blue-grey leaves, deeply veined and puckered, and short heads of very pale lilac flowers. Feed it well and it can reach a height of 90cm (3ft) and spread of 1.5m (5ft). *H. sieboldii* has lance-shaped leaves with a narrow white edge and grows to 45cm (18in). Hostas are ideally suited to light shade; use them in foliage combinations with ferns and bamboos to create a cool restful refuge in the garden. If you have to use pellets to control slugs and snails, place them under the leaves in the pot away from pets.

IMPATIENS (BUSY LIZZIE)
These bushy evergreen perennials with succulent stems and flat spurred flowers are effective if used sparingly. The reds tend to be from the blue end of the spectrum, making them difficult to use with true reds and yellow-reds. The pure white varieties give a very cool, fresh feel, enhanced by the plant's moist, fleshy quality. Quite different is *I. niamniamensis*, an upright fleshy-stemmed plant with red or yellow parrot-bill flowers. It makes an exciting addition to the backyard jungle.

INCARVILLEA
A genus that includes plants with very different characters, from the showy and exotic to the graceful and dainty. *I. delavayi* is an easy plant, 60cm (2ft) high, useful for giving a lush effect. From its clump of deeply divided, crinkly leaves arise stout erect stems holding aloft several robust, pink trumpet flowers. It benefits

Set against a backdrop of greenery, the intense bluey-red flowers of impatiens have an eyecatching brilliance.

from some protection in winter. In contrast, *I. sinensis* 'Cheron' has fine, fern-like foliage and more delicate, creamy-white flowers on scrambling stems 60cm (2ft) long. Treat it as tender. Grow it with *Solenopsis axillaris* to produce a misty, transparent effect.

LOBELIA TUPA

It is hard to imagine that this half-hardy perennial is related to the familiar annual lobelia. It can reach 90–150cm (3–5ft), and the stems, sprouting light green, downy leaves, are topped with a spike of curious two-lipped, red-brown flowers. Sombrely effective grown with *Stachys citrina* and *Coreopsis verticillata* 'Moonbeam'.

LOTUS BERTHELOTII

This evergreen has fine silvery leaves and striking scarlet flowers like upturned claws in summer. The soft, feathery stems will trail to 60–90cm (2–3ft), making this a good plant for hanging baskets. Use it with *Petasites paradoxus* for contrasting leaf texture and matching colour.

MELIANTHUS MAJOR

A magnificent grey-green foliage plant. The large leaves are deeply cut into numerous leaflets, each sharply toothed along the margin. Plants can reach 2–3m (6½–10ft) in height, but more often will attain only half that size in a container. They do not always flower when pot-grown but, given the foliage, that is of little consequence; they look stunning with the chocolate *Cosmos atrosanguineus*. Crushed leaves smell of a curious and not always pleasant mixture of rubber and peanut butter. Cut leggy growth back in spring.

MIMULUS AURANTIACUS

The soft colours of the flowers are the primary reason for growing this plant. Growth can be straggly, but it is usually self-supporting, growing to a height of 45–60cm (1½–2ft). The pale buff and pale apricot forms are ideal for adding lightness to a scheme. Soft orange *Begonia sutherlandii* and pale green *Helichrysum petiolare* 'Limelight' make good partners, as do pure blues and yellows.

MOLINIA CAERULEA 'Variegata'

An elegant and most useful grass, growing to 45cm (18in) high, with narrow arching leaves striped creamy yellow. Spikes of tiny purple flowers wave from the top of cream stems in late summer. It adds softness to a planting; try it with the blue-flowered *Felicia amelloides* or with *Trifolium repens* 'Purpurascens Quadrifolium'.

NEMESIA CAERULEA

A very pretty, bushy little plant, easy-going and cheerful, growing to 20cm (8in) and producing a cloud of small lilac flowers on an upright stem. It will flower up to the first hard frost, so shear off those flowers that are spent to encourage a new flush. *N. denticulata* 'Confetti' is similar but hardier, and its flowers have crimped petals which add to its charm. Delightful for creating a light feel and when planted with *Verbena* 'Loveliness' or *Oxalis vulcanicola*.

OPHIOPOGON PLANISCAPUS
'Nigrescens'

This black-leaved plant is a gem and an absolute boon to the container gardener. Its diminutive size, just 20cm (8in), belies the impact it can have. Leathery, shiny, narrow leaves sprout from easily divided tuberous roots. Black shiny berries in late summer are a bonus. Good with succulents, grey foliage and just about any flower colour.

ORIGANUM LAEVIGATUM

A sun-loving herbaceous perennial that grows to 45cm (18in) in height. From a compact clump of small grey leaves shoot wiry red stems branching into a misty spray of purple-pink flowers from midsummer onwards. It associates well with grey foliage, and is a good partner for the furry grey leaves and pale yellow flowers of *Stachys citrina* or the smaller-leaved *Lotus hirsutus*.

OSTEOSPERMUM

These plants produce large, daisy-like flowers that open in response to the sun. An ever-increasing number of varieties provide a range of colours that includes white, pink, blue, yellow and purple. Many have petals that are differently coloured on the reverse. Some have an upright habit, others are more spreading, but all make excellent container plants, giving a cheerful summery effect. Cuttings are easily rooted during late summer.
O. ecklonis 'Blue Streak' is an upright plant, 45cm (18in) high. Its white flowers have blue centres and are blue on the reverse. Also upright, *O.* 'Buttermilk', 60cm (2ft) high, has dark-eyed, soft yellow flowers. Both varieties create a fresh, cooling effect. *O. jucundum* is a low-growing spreading plant, 30cm (12in), which will spill out of a container. It produces soft

mauve flowers in good numbers during summer and autumn.

PELARGONIUM

Pelargoniums offer a very wide range of flower colours and leaf shapes, so much so that you could create startlingly varied displays using pelargoniums alone. Varieties whose flowers are less showy than those of traditional 'geraniums' more than make up for it with attractive, scented foliage. 'Mabel Grey', 45–60cm (1½–2ft) tall, has lemon-scented, deeply cut, stiff,

The natural affinity between red pelargoniums and clay pots guarantees stunning results.

rough leaves which give a very busy effect. 'Chocolate Peppermint', the most wonderful plant, reaches a height of 45–60cm (1½–2ft) and a spread of 60–90cm (2–3ft). Its large, shallow-lobed, rounded velvety leaves measure 15cm (6in) across and have a dark splash in the middle, and are spread around and out of the pot by thick hairy stems. The foliage has a strong scent of peppermint when crushed.
P. 'L'Elégante' is a variegated, ivy-leaved trailing pelargonium, growing to 60cm (2ft), with white-edged leaves which give the plant a succulent appearance. The pale mauve flowers are subdued enough to be a good complement to the busy foliage. Both *P. crispum* and *P.c.* 'Variegatum' are stiff, upright plants, 45–60cm (1½–2ft) tall, whose charm comes from the small, aromatic, crinkly foliage. *P.* 'Atomic Snowflake' – an awful name for a wonderful plant – grows 30cm (12in) high. Its mounds of pale, rounded leaves, gently variegated and scalloped, sit softly and comfortably at the edge of a planting.

PENSTEMON

Upright, shrubby plants, 45–60cm (1½–2ft) tall, with narrow, lance-shaped leaves. Their trumpet-shaped flowers, ranging from cherry red to dark purple, provide a wealth of colour from midsummer until late autumn. When pot-grown, penstemons are best treated as half-hardy. Plants are easily propagated from late summer cuttings. 'Snow Storm' has white trumpet flowers, 'Midnight' very dark violet-purple. 'Alice Hindley' – a dream of a plant – has large, dusty lavender and white flowers which combine beautifully with silvery foliage. 'Stapleford Gem' ('Sour Grapes') is a curious mix of blue and grey-purple.

PETASITES

Excellent foliage plants, with large, bold leaves. Far too invasive to let loose in the garden, but tamed in a pot, *P. japonicus* 'Variegatus' is an exciting and majestic plant. When well nourished, the round leaves, splashed and streaked with an irregular yellow variegation, can reach 60cm (2ft) or more across. Try it with a large grass such as *Helictotrichon sempervirens* or the bamboo *Pleioblastus auricomus*. It can also be used to stunning effect in very large hanging baskets. *P. palmatus* is a vigorous grower, although it reaches only 30–45cm (12–18in), with jagged-fingered leaves which give it a unique character. Use on its own or as a foil for lighter, airy plants. The leaves of *P. paradoxus* are silver, almost white, when young, while older leaves are green above, intense silver below. At 30cm (12in) in height, it is a less vigorous species than those mentioned above, but is a useful plant where plain but effective foliage is needed.

PHORMIUM (NEW ZEALAND FLAX)

These evergreens are extremely useful in providing a bold vertical line and giving structure to a planting. If, faced with planting a large container, you are wondering where to start, place a large phormium in the centre to spark off ideas. *P. tenax* 'Purpureum' has stiff, upright, sword-shaped, purple-green leaves. It is potentially a tall plant, to 2.5m (8ft), but

will remain smaller in a container. *P.t.* 'Bronze Baby' is a smaller version, growing to 60cm (2ft), with wine-red leaves. *Melianthus major, Petasites japonicus* 'Variegatus' and *Argyranthemum frutescens* all make good companions.

RHODOCHITON ATROSANGUINEUS

This classy climber, with dark purple, hanging tubular flowers, will reach a height of 2–3m (6½–10ft). Left unsupported, it will trail. Although perennial, it can easily be raised from seed each year. It makes a novel plant for hanging baskets, and the foliage of *Artemisia* 'Powis Castle', *Helichrysum petiolare* or *Plectranthus coleoides* 'Variegatus' all help show off the flowers.

SALVIA

This vast family encompasses a wide variety of plants of diverse sizes and colours, many of which are useful to the container gardener. *S. coccinea* 'Cherry Blossom' ('Coral Nymph') is a light and graceful salvia, 30cm (12in) high, with open tiers of white and pink flowers. Treat it as an annual and grow with *Petunia* 'Chiffon Morn' or *Pelargonium* 'Preston Park'. *S. confertiflora* is a large and distinctive plant, growing to a height of 1.2m (4ft). Its green leaves with brown undersides and small, red-brown flowers packed on a tall, red, velvety flower spike make an impressive sight in late summer. Use it with strong foliage plants like zantedeschia, or go the opposite way and surround it with the frothy frizz of white *Argyrantheum foeniculaceum*. *S. patens*

has flowers of a most penetrating gentian blue. It grows to 45cm (18in) high and from early sown seed it can be flowering by midsummer. A simple planting using *S.p.* 'White Trophy' and the pale blue *S.p.* 'Cambridge Blue' makes a very effective display. *S. farinacea* is an upright plant with spikes of small violet-blue flowers on velvety stems, 45–75cm (1½–2½ft) high. The variety 'Strata' has violet-blue flowers with a white calyx, producing an appealing two-tone effect, and foliage with a grey sheen. Treat it as an annual. 'Alba' has mealy white flowers which associate well with *Helichrysum petoliare* and *Senecio maritima* 'Silver Dust'. *S. cacaliifolia* is a vigorous plant, 45–60cm (1½–2ft) high, ideal for trailing over the sides of pots. It has royal blue, narrow, tubular flowers and heart-shaped, finely hairy leaves. Mix it in with other intense colours or with white agapanthus. *S. elegans* is a sprawling plant, growing 45–60cm (1½–2ft), with charming, bright red tubular flowers and leaves that smell of pineapple when crushed. Easily rooted from cuttings taken during the summer, it is most useful for large containers where its vigour can be accommodated against the bold broad leaves of zantedeschias or *Pelargonium* 'Chocolate Peppermint'.

SCAEVOLA AEMULA 'BLUE WONDER'

A trailing plant, growing 30–45cm (1–1½ft) long, and covered in small, fan-shaped, rich blue flowers. It is a durable plant that will flower until the frosts and is ideal for growing in hanging baskets where the flowering stems can be seen at their best.

SENECIO

A genus of plants whose leaves range from white felt to blue-grey succulent, through the green 'beads' of *S. rowleyanus*. *S. viravira* is a vigorous spreading plant with silvery white, much divided leaves, growing to a height of 45cm (1½ft) and a spread of 90cm (3ft) or more. The flowers are insignificant creamy tufts. It is happy to trail over the edge of containers or scramble up through stronger plants and may need pruning to prevent it over-running lesser plants. It makes a good foil for strong colours such as *Dahlia* 'Bishop of Llandaff' and *Phormium tenax* 'Purpureum'. *S. maritima* 'Silver Dust' is more compact and feathery, with a height and spread of 30cm (12in). Pinch out the weed-like flowerheads. For a filigree effect grow it with *Verbena bonariensis* and *Origanum laevigatum*.

SOLEIROLIA SOLEIROLII
(MIND-YOUR-OWN-BUSINESS)

A vigorous, spreading carpet of tiny leaves, 5cm (2in) high, making a neat 'ground cover' among other plants in pots but just as attractive on its own. It can be tamed with a pair of scissors. Although evergreen, it can be turned brown by frost. 'Argentea' has variegated leaves that give the plant a grey appearance. 'Aurea' has fresh yellow-green foliage.

SOLENOPSIS AXILLARIS

This dainty plant, reaching 20–30cm (8–12in) in height, has fine leaves and narrow-petalled, pale blue, star-shaped flowers. It has a slightly scrambling habit, but set among bolder plants it will have a softening effect. It provides plentiful amounts of seed. A related white variety is available.

SPHAERALCEA MUNROANA

Soft, hairy leaves provide the perfect setting for small, pink, mallow-like flowers which are produced all summer long. *S. munroana* will spread and hang delightfully from a hanging basket or windowbox, reaching 45cm (18in). Make the most of its gentle summery feel by growing it with similar charmers, such as *Tulbaghia violacea* or blue *Convolvulus sabatius*.

STACHYS CITRINA

A wonderful mix of soft, dusty grey, felted leaves and small, pale yellow flowers. Use it in small arrangements as a foil for brighter colours and as a contrast to glossy foliage. It grows 15–17cm (6–7in) high and dislikes winter wet.

TOLMIEA MENZIESII 'TAFF'S GOLD'
(PICK-A-BACK PLANT)

A decorative plant, growing up to 45cm (18in) tall, with mottled variegation on ivy-shaped leaves and intriguing tiny green and brown flowers in spring, which should be snipped off as they go over. Ideal in dappled shade where it seems almost to glow, and good with yellows and for adding light to an arrangement. Pendulous yellow begonias, white or blue lobelias and *Trifolium repens* 'Purpureum Quadrifolium' all make good companions. It is easily propagated from the young plants that form at the base of the leaf.

TRADESCANTIA

These evergreen trailing plants with oval, pointed leaves are useful for hanging baskets or when allowed to scramble around among more substantial plants. They grow to 15cm (6in) high and will trail almost indefinitely, and are easily propagated from cuttings. *T. zebrina* has dark leaves with glistening stripes which lighten the overall effect. *T. fluminensis* 'Variegata' is similar in form, but its leaves are light green and variegated, giving a spring freshness to an arrangement.

TROPAEOLUM

A genus of brightly coloured plants that includes the familiar nasturtium. All tropaeolums make equally good trailers or climbers and the abundance of flowers in warm colours manage never to look gaudy or garish. One rule, however: do not use them with reds at the blue end of the spectrum. *T. peregrinum* is a dainty, yellow-flowered climber with pretty, lobed leaves. It is a tender perennial best treated as an annual and grows to a height of 1.5–2m (5–6½ft). *T. tuberosum* is a climber of considerable distinction with grey-green, gently lobed leaves. It will climb 2–3m (6½–10ft) and the flowers, a blend of yellow, orange and red with a long spur, are held aloft on long stems, giving an exotic look. Overwinter the tubers in a frost-free place. There are several varieties of the vigorous and showy *T. majus* (nasturtium), both compact and trailing. The colours of

Argyranthemum gracile 'Chelsea Girl' and Osteospermum 'Pink Whirls'.

ZANTEDESCHIA AETHEOPICA
(ARUM LILY)

The arum lily has good architectural qualities of leaf and flower. Erect, arrow-shaped leaves on stout stems and white spathes are produced in early summer. After flowering, the leaves maintain their quality. Plants do not always need to be kept wet and will tolerate a few degrees of frost. Use with other bold foliage to create a sumptuous planting with a tropical feel.

BULBS

ALLIUM

These onion relatives range in colour from white and yellow through to blue and purple. One of the most striking varieties is *A. cristophii*, which has large round heads of star-like purple flowers in summer and grows 30–60cm (12–24in) tall. It produces a marvellous effect coming up through *Helichrysum petiolare* 'Limelight'.

CROCUS

Growing just 2.5–8cm (1–3in) tall, these cheerful, early spring-flowering plants are ideal in permanent plantings to start the season and, densely planted in small pots, provide bright splashes of colour. After flowering, the grassy foliage is unobtrusive. Two distinctive varieties are *C. chrysanthus* 'Cream Beauty', a warm cream, warmed still further by orange

Vigorous growth and abundant bright flowers make **Tropaeolum majus** *one of the most cheerful container plants.*

these annuals range from pale yellow 'Peach Melba' to the sultry dark crimson flowers and dark foliage of 'Empress of India'. 'Alaska' is a bushy variety with leaves irregularly splashed cream. The bushy varieties will grow to 20–30cm (8–12in), the trailing varieties 1–2m (3–6½ft).

TULBAGHIA VIOLACEA

A late season delight with narrow foliage and delicate, dainty heads of pink flowers on 45cm (18in) stems. The grassy foliage looks particularly good with black *Ophiopogon planiscapus* 'Nigrescens'. It will tolerate a degree or two of frost.

VERBENA

These colourful plants – many of which are deliciously scented – have a long flowering season. Deadhead regularly to encourage new flower buds. 'Silver Anne' is a spreading perennial with small, serrated leaves and large, rounded heads of small pink fragrant flowers all summer. 'Loveliness' has good heads of lilac flowers and a lovely scent. It will flower until the frosts. Both varieties grow to a height and spread of 45cm (18in) or more. *V. bonariensis* is very different. Its narrow, sparse, rigidly upright stems, growing to 1.5m (5ft) high, are topped with tufts of purple-blue flowers from midsummer through autumn. It is most useful for growing through more lax plants, or for defining the vertical line of a planting. Take cuttings to perpetuate named varieties. Good summer companions are

stigmas, and *C.c.* 'Blue Pearl', a cool
lavender-blue with a yellow centre.

GALANTHUS (SNOWDROP)

Snowdrops make charming highlights
among dark foliage. Try them with
the beetroot-red leaves of *Bergenia
purpurascens*. Early spring-flowering
plants, they grow from 10–30cm (4–12in).
G. elwesii is chunky, with broad, strap-like
glaucous leaves, while *G.* 'Atkinsii' is
graceful, dainty and single-flowered.

GALTONIA

This hardy bulb sends up tall stems,
90–120cm (3–4ft) high and hung with
substantial white bells, to make a stately
plant for late summer effect. Plant it to
come up through zantedeschia or
melianthus. *G. viridiflora* is slightly
smaller and has bells of cool, pale green.

MUSCARI BOTRYOIDES (GRAPE HYACINTH)

Very common but reliable and attractive
blue-flowered plants which flower in spring
and grow to a height of about 10cm (4in).
Mix them with evergreens or plant them in
a pot of their own. 'Album' is the white
form – very hardy and extremely classy.

NARCISSUS (DAFFODIL)

Tough and ideal for container growing,
daffodils will cheer up the dreariest corner
of the garden. Heights range from 8–45cm
(3–18in) and colours from rich egg-yolk
yellow to glistening white. Try mixing pale
varieties with clipped box or yew for a

sophisticated effect. 'Thalia', 38cm (15in)
high, has delicate, pale yellow flowers best
seen against a dark evergreen background.
'Tête à Tête' is a dainty plant, 23cm (9in)
high, with small, richly coloured flowers,
two or three to a stem. It is ideal for a
spring-flowering windowbox.

TULIPA (TULIP)

Tulips come in an almost bewildering
range of shapes and sizes, but all are
suitable for container-growing. Parrot
tulips, 45–60cm (18–24in) tall, have large
flowers and fringed and flared petals, and
make a particularly flamboyant display.
T. 'White Triumphator' is a white lily-
flowered tulip, growing to 60cm (2ft), with
reflexed petals and considerable style. It
flowers in late spring. *T. batalinii* 'Bright
Gem' is a small, early spring-flowering
tulip with soft-yellow petals washed with
orange, set among blue-tinted leaves. It
will reach 10–30cm (4–12in).

SUCCULENTS

AEONIUM ARBOREUM
'ARNOLD SCHWARZKOPFF'

Shiny black rosettes of succulent leaves
make this branching perennial a striking
plant, either on its own or as part of a 'dry
garden' arrangement. It will grow up to
90cm (3ft) tall.

AGAVE AMERICANA (CENTURY PLANT)

Although agaves eventually become
enormous plants, young plants can be

contained in pots for many years at more
manageable heights of 15–75cm (6–30in).
Its large rosettes of tough, fleshy leaves
each finish with a very sharp spine – notice
the pattern of spines that each leaf presses
into the other. There are two variegated
forms, one striped yellow, the other grey.

CEROPEGIA WOODII

An easily grown and intriguing trailing
plant, hanging to 60–90cm (2–3ft), with
heart-shaped, silver-green mottled leaves
on wiry stems and curious, un-showy pink
flowers. Older specimens develop dense
swags of stems. It is an unusual plant for
adding a vertical line to a planting and
unique in its colouring.

ECHEVERIA

Echeverias have distinctive rosettes of
fleshy leaves which rest on the ground,
some softly hairy (*E. pulvinata*), others
with wavy or crinkled leaf margins
(*E.* 'Aquarius'), and ranging in colour from
flesh pink to purple-blue. Exotic pink and
yellow flowers are produced along erect
stems, ranging in height from 5–45cm
(2–18in). Mix them with other dry-looking
plants such as *Lotus hirsutus*, *Lotus
maculatus*, *Festuca glauca* and *Ceropegia
woodii*, or try them with lush foliage plants
such as *Nemesia caerulea*, *Fuchsia
procumbens* and cultivars of *Begonia rex*.

SEDUM

Hardy and possessing considerable
character, sedums are good plants for
the front of a planting. *S. maximum*

'Atropurpureum' has smooth, fleshy leaves of dark maroon and flat heads of densely packed, small red flowers which give the plant a sombre, heavy feel. It combines well with cheerier and lighter plants, such as pink *Sphaeralcea munroana*, and will reach a height of 45cm (18in) or so. S. 'Bertram Anderson' is a small plant, 10cm (4in) high, with wonderful deep purple foliage and ruby-red flowers.

SENECIO KLEINIA

A vigorous spreading succulent with leaves resembling juicy blue pencils covered in a grey bloom. It is tolerant of being grown in a wide range of conditions and with a diverse selection of plants. Use with

The characterful flowers of echeverias will complement any planting scheme.

hairy-leaved plants that contrast with its smoothness, or let it scramble with *Tradescantia zebrina*.

ANNUALS AND BIENNIALS

LAGURUS OVATUS (HARE'S-TAIL GRASS)

A curious little annual grass with soft 'hare's tails' flowerheads at the top of fine stems 45cm (18in) high. It is easily propagated from seed. Try it with *Begonia rex* cultivars or succulent crassulas.

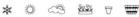

LOBELIA ERINUS

One of the cheeriest, most useful and, if looked at closely, most beautifully flowered plants. Low and narrow-leaved with compact or trailing habit, they are covered

in dainty flowers right through summer to autumn. The bushy varieties reach a height and spread of 15cm (6in), trailing varieties 23cm (9in). Plants range in colour from red, pink and blue to lilac and white and are invaluable as fillers in all plantings, covering the compost until the larger plants spread out. The 'Cascade' series of trailers is particularly useful in hanging baskets. They are suitable for mixing with almost any other plants, but lilac 'Cascade' with *Verbena* 'Loveliness' or *Nemesia caerulea* looks particularly striking.

NEMESIA 'KLM'

A small potful of this cheery little annual with its sky-blue and white flowers makes an eye-catching display. Plants reach a sprawling 23–30cm (9–12in).

PETUNIA

Though breeders have improved petunias' resistance to bad weather, the plants will perform better if given some shelter from the wind, reaching heights of 30–45cm (12–18in). Many of the colours available are quite harsh and difficult to use, in particular the striped varieties. However, two useful single colours are soft pink 'Chiffon Morn' and pure white, of which there are several varieties. Always try to buy single colours rather than mixed to give yourself more control over the planting scheme. Try combining white petunias with *Tolmiea menziesii* 'Taff's Gold' and *Hakonechloa macra* 'Aureola', and 'Chiffon Morn' with *Pelargonium* 'Atomic Snowflake'.

INDEX

Page numbers in italics indicate illustrations.

INDEX

ACKNOWLEDGMENTS

Author's acknowledgments
I would like to give my special thanks to Valerie Christie who typed the manuscript, and to Mr and Mrs R Paice for their permission to use their garden at Bourton House, Bourton-on-the-Hill, Moreton-in-Marsh, Gloucestershire, for photography. Thanks also to Keith Finlay of Rowborough Farm, Stretton-on-Fosse, Warwickshire for the wicker baskets photographed on pages 60-1, and to Kate Langley for letting us use her home to photograph the silvered windowbox planting project on pages 74-5.

Publisher's acknowledgments
The publisher would like to thank the following photographers and organizations for their kind permission to reproduce the photographs in this book:
2-3 Juliette Wade (Sparrowhall); 5 Camera Press; 6-7 S & O Mathews (Upper House); 9 J C Mayer - G Le Scanff (Chaumont-sur-Loire, Laurence Claude); 12 Vincent Motte (Lafourcade); 13 Gary Rogers; 14 Gary Rogers; 15 John Glover (Vann, Surrey); 19 Brigitte Thomas (Walda Pairon); 20 J C Mayer - G Le Scanff (La Closerie, Normandy); 21 Andrew Lawson (Gothic House); 22 Clive Nichols (Bourton House); 23 Marijke Heuff (Hadspen); 24 Andrew Lawson (Pots & Pithoi, Sussex); 25 The Garden Picture Library (Marijke Heuff); 26 left The Garden Picture Library (John Glover); 26-7 Michèle Lamontagne; 27 right The Garden Picture Library (Marijke Heuff); 28 left John Glover (Vann, Surrey); 28 right Juliette Wade (Will Giles); 29 Brigitte Thomas (Timothy Vaughan); 30 J C Mayer - G Le Scanff (La Closerie, Normandy); 31 The Garden Picture Library (Lorna Rose); 32 Jerry Harpur (Sonny Garcia, J Di Faustino); 33 Paul Williams (Bourton House); 34-5 Jerry Harpur (Anne Alexander-Sinclair); 34 left Clive Nichols (Bourton House); 35 right Andrew Lawson (Barter's Farm Nurseries); 36 Clive Nichols (The Old Rectory, Berks); 37 Clive Nichols (Bourton House); 38 Anne Hyde; 51 Clive Nichols (Bourton House); 52 Jerry Harpur (Bourton House); 53 Marianne Majerus; 55 Brigitte Thomas (Jane Newdick); 56 Michèle Lamontagne; 57 right Michèle Lamontagne; 57 left J C Mayer - G Le Scanff (Les Forrières du Bosc); 58-9 S & O Mathews; 66 Michèle Lamontagne; 67 Charles Mann (C Butte); 68 John Glover; 69 below Andrew Lawson (Bourton House); 69 top J C Mayer - G Le Scanff; 70 left John Glover (Chelsea Flower Show 1992); 70 right Andrew Lawson; 71 John Glover; 72 John Glover; 73 Andrew Lawson (John Brookes); 80 Derek St Romaine (Chelsea Flower Show 1995); 81 Andrew Lawson (Bourton House); 82 Clive Nichols (Bourton House); 84 The Garden Picture Library (Marijke Heuff); 87 The Garden Picture Library (Marijke Heuff, Mien Ruys Garden); 88 John Glover; 91 The Garden Picture Library (J S Sira).

The photographs on the following pages were taken specially for Conran Octopus by Georgia Glynn-Smith: 1, 8, 10, 11, 16, 17, 18, 39, 40-51, 54, 60-5, 74-9.

The publisher would also like to thank Helen Woodhall.
Index compiled by Indexing Specialists, Hove, East Sussex BN3 2DJ.